Portland Stair Walks

I'D RATHER BE READING BOOKS FROM

Microcosm.Pub

2752 N WILLIAMS AVE · PORTLAND, OR 97227

Portland Stair Walks

Explore Portland, Oregon's Public Stairways

PLUS HIDDEN PATHS AND PEDESTRIAN/BIKE BRIDGES

Laura O. Foster

Microcosm Publishing
Portland, OR

Portland Stair Walks: Explore Portland, Oregon's Public Stairways

Copyright © 2019 by Laura O. Foster

This edition © Microcosm Publishing, 2019

First Edition, 3,000 copies, First published April, 2019

Photos by the author, except pages 50, 70, and 128, courtesy of Portland Archives

Maps by Lisa Brower of GreenEye Design

Cover by Trista Vercher and Joe Biel

Book design by Joe Biel

ISBN 978-1-62106-345-2

This is Microcosm #257

For a catalog, write or visit:
Microcosm Publishing
2752 N Williams Ave.
Portland, OR 97227
(503)799-2698
Microcosm.Pub

If you bought this on Amazon, I'm so sorry because you could have gotten it cheaper and supported a small, independent publisher at MICROCOSM.PUB

Global labor conditions are bad, and our roots in industrial Cleveland in the 70s and 80s made us appreciate the need to treat workers right. Therefore, our books are MADE IN THE USA and printed on post-consumer paper.

To join the ranks of high-class stores that feature Microcosm titles, talk to your local rep: In the U.S. *Como (Atlantic), Fujii (Midwest), Travelers West (Pacific), Manda in Canada, Turnaround in Europe, and Baker & Taylor Publisher Services* for other countries.

Library of Congress Cataloging-in-Publication Data

Names: Foster, Laura O.
Title: Portland stair walks : explore Portland, Oregon's public stairways /
    Laura O. Foster.
Description: Portland, Oregon : Microcosm Publishing, [2019] | Includes index.
Identifiers: LCCN 2018039079 | ISBN 9781621063452 (pbk.)
Subjects: LCSH: Portland (Or.)--Guidebooks. |
    Staircases--Oregon--Portland--Guidebooks. |
    Walking--Oregon--Portland--Guidebooks.
Classification: LCC F884.P83 F676 2019 | DDC 917.95/4904--dc23
LC record available at https://lccn.loc.gov/2018039079

MICROCOSM · PUBLISHING

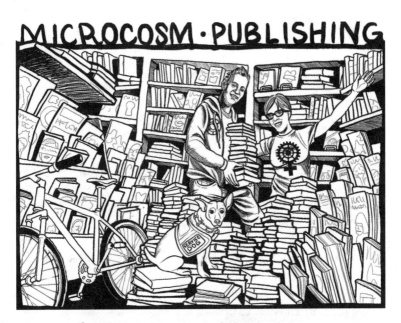

About the Publisher

MICROCOSM PUBLISHING is Portland's most diversified publishing house and distributor with a focus on the colorful, authentic, and empowering. Our books and zines have put your power in your hands since 1996, equipping readers to make positive changes in their lives and in the world around them. Microcosm emphasizes skill-building, showing hidden histories, and fostering creativity through challenging conventional publishing wisdom with books and bookettes about DIY skills, food, bicycling, gender, self-care, and social justice. What was once a distro and record label was started by Joe Biel in his bedroom and has become among the oldest independent publishing houses in Portland, OR. We are a politically moderate, centrist publisher in a world that has inched to the right for the past 80 years.

Contents

▪▪▪▪▪▪

Using This Book

WHERE DO PORTLAND'S STAIRS TAKE YOU? To little-known paths, dead-ends in name only, unexpected angles framing the city, and nooks hidden from Google Earth. As you climb an outdoor staircase, rewards increase with each step—views of two rivers, 16 river bridges, and four volcanoes with green buttes clustered at their flanks. Staircases lift you to these vistas, but also reward a contemplative walker with micro views: peeks into terraced backyards and, more minutely, into the fascinating life on the steps themselves.

This book uses Portland's hundreds of public staircases, hidden pathways, and pedestrian/bike bridges to get you out, exploring, being delighted at how creative Portlanders can be, discovering changes to our parks and natural areas, and enjoying the food and drink we love to talk about when we're not actually eating and drinking.

If you do all the 18 walks in this book, you'll have climbed or descended 142 staircases, trod 22 hidden paths, crossed 26 bridges, emerged from 2 tunnels (one in ground and one in the air), walked a floating sidewalk, and sailed over a neighborhood on an aerial tram. You'll also have explored a few beaches, stood on an island, visited three creeks, and maybe taken a swim in the river.

Use *Portland Stair Walks* as a guidebook or armchair travelogue. Read a route, plan a bit, call a friend, and get out. An urban walking or biking exploration makes the best kind of date. Go with a friend, an old spouse, a new lover, or a child of any age. There's always much to laugh over, wonder about, and appreciate. Portlanders are a creative lot with our landscapes and home ornamentation, rarely content with poodle-clipped trees and a few pots of geraniums. A walk in Portland is my therapy of choice, almost always resulting in warm feelings toward my fellow humans.

And don't wait for the rain to stop. The most magical walks can be on misty days. Colors really pop against grey skies. The occasional deluge? Get out with your boots and umbrella and look for staircases turned into Class V rapids. Slosh a bit, Gene Kelly-style, in a puddle or curb lake, and bring a stick to clear the storm drains. Views are grand on clear days: macro and mighty. But cloudy, misty, and even torrential days showcase the small treasures at your feet.

My stair-loving ways have been featured on OPB's *Oregon Field Guide* in an episode called "Portland Stairways." That often-repeated episode garners lots of social media commentary, and was the impetus for this, a reconceived version of my first stairs book, with new stories and many more routes.

Here's what's inside:

MAPPED STAIR WALKS

Spend a day being a tourist in Portland. Pick one of the six walks, from 3 to 6.5 miles and from 366 to 1,256 stairs. Each route starts with an area orientation, map, and quick guide to directions. After this come more detailed directions interlaced with photos and stories. You'll pick up nuggets about local geology, history, native trees, heritage trees or infrastructure, like that massive tower atop Healy Heights. The layers of backstory within a landscape are unpacked with enough detail to add to your stash of Portland lore, but not so much to turn this into a history book.

Each quadrant is covered. Each stair walk takes you by places to eat and drink, usually in an old streetcar-era commercial district.

MAP KEY
━ ROUTE
⋯⋯ STAIRS
═ HIDDEN PATH
– – TRAILS
▨ PARKS/GREENSPACE
🚻 PUBLIC RESTROOMS
🍴 FOOD/DRINK
🚏 TRANSIT STOP

THIS MAP KEY IS FOR THE SIX MAPS IN THE MAPPED STAIR WALKS SECTION.

URBAN FORAGES FOR MORE STAIRS, HIDDEN PATHS, AND PEDESTRIAN BRIDGES

In this section are 12 more routes, from 2 to 17 miles. Some have just a few staircases, others have you climbing 800+ stairs. Several routes are good for biking (many urban staircases have gutters for bikes to roll on). Essentially, these forages use stairs, paths, bridges and tunnels as an excuse to go sniffing around the city's folds and furrows. Along the way, you'll find intriguing businesses and other fascinating places occupying their city niches, just waiting for curious walkers to find them. And food and drink, a sine qua non of every urban walk.

Directions in this section are detailed enough to forego a map. A map app may be useful, but digital maps get tedious when you want the bigger picture. I recommend the free, paper walking and biking maps from the City of Portland. There's one for each quadrant. Order from Portland Bureau of Transportation at PortlandOregon.gov.

RIVER BRIDGES, JOINING THE CITIZEN STEWARDS

Other sections list Portland's 16 bridges, their stairs and pedestrian access, and tell you where to connect with volunteers who shine up various corners of the city.

Public Transit Versus Driving to the Start of Walks

If you're not already using public transit, use the bus or train to get to the starting points. An urban exploration is so much more enjoyable when you don't have to worry about where to park, or about overstaying your welcome in your parking space, or even about returning to the exact place you started.

Driving in Portland is increasingly unpleasant, and finding parking even less fun, so get yourself an all-day TriMet pass and forget about it.

PortlandStairWalks.com

Find more stair info on the book's website, including a complete list of the City's public stairs, stair vocabulary (with photos), more stories of places along the routes, and updates regarding trail closures or changes. Also find info on new pedestrian bridges, and other ways to get out and explore the city on foot or by bike.

CITIZEN-BUILT STAIRS ALONG SW 25TH AVENUE, SOUTH OF BEAVERTON-HILLSDALE HWY

■.■.■.■.■.■

Mapped Stair Walks

THE SIX ROUTES IN THIS SECTION MEANDER ON THEIR WAY to maximal coverage of staircases, viewpoints, and other intriguing places. Do them all and you'll have conquered 70 staircases, crossed four bridges, and discovered 11 hidden paths.

Quadrant	Stair Walk	Miles	Number of Staircases	Number of Stair steps*
North and Northwest	Cathedral Park to Linnton	3, one-way	5 to 11	432 to 1,256
Northeast	Alameda Ridge	6.5	11	838
Northwest	Slabtown, Nob Hill, and Westover Terraces	6	15 to 17	983 to 1,197
Southeast	Mt. Tabor	4.5	11 or 12	633 to 719
Southwest	Hillsdale to Council Crest Park	4.6	6 or 7	366 to 406
Southwest	Portland Heights	3.6 to 5	12	529

*Optional stairs require a descent and ascent.

Cathedral Park to Linnton

THIS 3-MILE, ONE-WAY STAIR WALK RATES HIGH on covering intriguing ground, with a few unpleasant bits that make the good stuff all the sweeter. It crosses Portland's most photographed bridge, the St. Johns Bridge. Headphones are a good idea for the bridge traverse. It's scenic but loud.

On the St. Johns side, you're in Cathedral Park, climbing a staircase much used for marriages under the bridge's Gothic-arched piers. After crossing the bridge into Linnton, you weave in and out of four isolated micro-neighborhoods, each enveloped by forested creek valleys. Staircases abound; the route takes you to 11, with about 500 feet of elevation gain. Linnton's streets, terraced into steep hillsides, were built before street building codes. They're usually narrow, sidewalk-free, and curbless, creating a fascinating back-of-the-beyond feel. The neighborhood's remote and unpolished vibe, despite proximity to Hwy 30, is part of its charm.

The stair walk ends, satisfyingly, at a historic tavern, the Lighthouse. Retrace your steps after lunch. Or ride TriMet's No. 16 bus back to the start. It runs every 40 minutes from NW 107th and Hwy 30 (Stop 5357). Ride 10 minutes to N Ivanhoe and Baltimore; then walk six blocks back to the start.

Not all Portland streets are congested

MAP SCALE

0 MILES 1/8

Pier Park

SMITH ST

CENTRAL ST

KELLOGG ST

ST LOUIS AVE

ST JOHNS AVE

LOMBARD ST

IVANHOE ST

SYRACUSE ST

WILLAMETTE BLVD

DECATUR ST

EDISON ST

BRADFORD ST

LOMBARD ST

RENO AVE

BALTIMORE AVE

PHILADELPHIA AVE

BURLINGTON AVE

PRINCETON ST

EDISON ST

CRAWFORD ST

WATER POLLUTION CONTROL LAB

Cathedral Park

1

2

ST JOHNS BRIDGE

TERMINAL RD

CATHEDRAL PARK

Willamette River

3

BRIDGE AVE

SPRINGVILLE RD

4

GERMANTOWN RD

OLD SPRINGVILLE RD

ST HELENS RD

HARBOR BLVD

ROSEWAY AVE

ELVA AVE

TOLINDA TRAIL

Forest Park

30

5

HOGE AVE

MACKAY AVE

WILARK AVE

FIRELANE 9

LINNTON

FRONT AVE

109TH AVE

10TH AVE

FORMER LINNTON PLYWOOD MILL

1ST ST

2ND ST

3RD ST

5TH ST

WATER TANK

LINNTON TRAIL

6

N

Neighborhood CATHEDRAL PARK, LINNTON

DIRECTIONS: THE QUICK GUIDE

1 ■ ■ Begin near the Cathedral Park boat ramp, at the foot of N Baltimore Avenue. From the restrooms, follow the paved path toward and then away from the Willamette River.

■ ■ Where the path forks, keep left to walk uphill, passing the concrete anchorage for the bridge's cables. Cross a street; at another fork, take neither path but walk across the grass toward the stagelike area between bridge piers, then climb the park's famous stairs.

■ ■ Cross Edison, then veer left to continue uphill under the bridge on Philadelphia.

2 ■ ■ Turn right on Syracuse and then immediately right to start the 0.7-mile walk across the bridge.

3 ■ ■ Once across, turn right on Bridge Avenue.

4 ■ ■ At the Hwy 30 stoplight, cross Bridge Avenue, then turn left to walk a sidewalk and elevated sidewalk along Hwy 30.

■ ■ At Harbor Blvd, turn left and hairpin up the hill. Follow Harbor west, then veer right onto Roseway.

■ ■ Follow Roseway to beyond the garage at 9663; descend 67 stairs to Hwy 30. Turn left, walking the sidewalk briefly, then turn left at Hoge.

5 ■ ■ At the X-shaped intersection, keep far right, to walk on Wilark. Just past the last home/garage, descend 42 stairs to an elevated sidewalk. Turn left onto Hwy 30.

6 ▪▪ Come to a staircase. Climb. At the top, walk right to the end of 2nd. Walk out 2nd and veer left on 3rd Court, following it to 3rd Street and the top of 176 stairs. Descend to Hwy 30.

▪▪ Have lunch at the Lighthouse, then catch the bus at 107th and Hwy 30.

BARGE, FROM ST. JOHN'S BRIDGE. FOREST PARK AND THE FORMER ST. JOHN'S FERRY TERMINUS IN BACKGROUND

1 **Begin near the Cathedral Park Boat Ramp, at the foot of N Baltimore Avenue. Park in the adjacent car (not the boat) lot. From the restroom, follow the paved path toward the river and bridge; check out the beach and the floating dock under the bridge.** You're on the banks of the Willamette River, the nation's thirteenth largest river, by volume. From the confluence of two forks of the river near Springfield, Oregon, the Willamette flows 187 miles north, meeting the Columbia River 5.8 miles from where you're standing. The Willamette's watershed drains nearly 12 percent of Oregon, and 70 percent of Oregonians live in its valley. It's one of the nation's few north-flowing rivers.

Here you're on the Lower Willamette, i.e., the river downstream of Willamette Falls. The channel here, in what is called the Portland Harbor, is mechanically dredged to 40 feet deep for commercial ships. Before dredging, most of the Lower Willamette was less than 20 feet deep, in places low enough to wade across during the summer. The Portland Harbor is a Superfund site, part of a federal program to clean up severely polluted land and waterways. Chemical pollutants that infest the river's sediments are the result of over a century of heavy industry during an era of little environmental protections. Dumping of toxins was allowed and practiced.

Despite the degraded sediments, the river is clean enough to swim in, after decades of infrastructure improvements (such as the Big Pipe project) and restrictions on effluents. Water temps reach around 70 degrees in August and early September. The Human Access Project encourages Portlanders to take back our river, and offers guidelines for safe swimming at places like Cathedral Park, where the river banks in some places retain some resemblance to their natural state. There's nothing better than jumping into your own river on a hot August day after a bike ride. The water is silky and clear.

When facing the river, downstream (to the right) was the site of furious ship-building during WWI. Eighty wood-hulled ships were built at the Grant Smith-Porter Ship Company here from 1917 to 1919. St. Johns was also a locus of warship construction during WWII, one of three Kaiser shipyards in Portland and Vancouver.

After visiting the riverbank, come back to the path as it curves away from the river or just cross the lawn, heading to the brown steel sculpture in the grass. Poke your finger into the 40-foot-long "Drawing on the River" and listen to the results. The shapes at its ends echo hulls of the warships built here, and the body of the sculpture is suspended, like the bridge. Artist Donald Fels worked with fabricators at Peninsula Iron Works, the red-roofed buildings on the left you're about to pass. The art dates from 2008.

Peninsula Iron Works has been here since 1917; it's a machine shop that began by servicing the wood products industry. In WWII it converted to wartime production, producing 1.5 million hand grenade casings. Now it fabricates or repairs equipment for steel mills and rock crushers, among other jobs.

Where the path forks, keep left to walk uphill, passing a massive, beautiful concrete anchorage for the bridge's cables. Cross a street and now you're climbing. At another fork, take neither path but walk into the grass toward the stagelike area between bridge piers—a wedding venue. You will be possibly the one-millionth person who takes photos from here.

Walk up the 41 stairs that brides walk down, cross Edison, then veer left to continue uphill under the bridge on Philadelphia. Homes pre-date the bridge—some from the 1880s. I wonder what their owners felt when they saw this urban colossus rise up across the street from their front porches. The bridge was completed in 1931. It is, most agree, the state's most beautiful bridge.

2 **Turn right on Syracuse and then immediately right, to start the 0.7-mile walk across the bridge.** Views, as you encounter them:

Treetop/rooftop views over the neighborhood: nice yards!

Tanks across the river are part of the 5-mile-long Linnton Energy Cluster of oil, gas, diesel, jet fuel and liquefied natural gas. Almost all of the fossil fuel consumed in Oregon passes through the tanks or underground pipelines here. The Energy Cluster runs from the Guild's Lake Industrial Sanctuary to the tip of Sauvie Island. It's also traversed by rail lines, a U.S. highway, and electrical transmission lines, and dotted with electrical substations.

To the left is downtown Portland and the 1912 Railroad Bridge, 1 mile upriver from the St. Johns Bridge.

Beyond the red-roofed Peninsula Iron Works is the Port of Portland's Terminal 4, where new Toyotas from Japan roll off ships onto American pavement. The terminal's seven ship berths and 262-acres receive autos, steel, forest products, and dry and liquid bulk products.

The flat ground at Terminal 4 is landfill that buried wetlands and side channels, and ground where Native Americans camped. A transient camper in 1806 was William Clark, of the Lewis and Clark Expedition. He had heard of a large tributary of the Columbia that flowed in from the south. During a weeklong camp in today's Washougal, Clark left the expedition and investigated the mouth of that river, the Willamette. This site is as far upriver as he went before turning around.

Forest Park is the organic green balm rising over the complicated river scene. A wilderness that runs along the east flank of the Tualatin Mountains, from the crests down to Hwy 30, Forest Park came into being in 1948 after most of its timber had been logged off. Now well into its second growth, the forest is in places primeval. Slopes are steep, 20 percent or more in most areas, and all but a few of the park's many creeks hurry down the steep slopes in winter, and vanish in summer.

MARRIAGE SPOT, UNDER THE ST. JOHN'S BRIDGE IN CATHEDRAL PARK

Look behind: on clear days Mt. Adams is nicely framed between the bridge towers.

On the west bank, look for a tiny road winding up from the river, to the right of the white warehouse; originally called Ferry Road, it led to the western terminus of the St. Johns Ferry that operated until this bridge opened in 1931. The ferry and bridge were on the historic route of fur trappers. In the 1820s and 1830s, they trapped beaver in the Tualatin Valley (now Beaverton, Tigard and Hillsboro), and packed the pelts up and over the Tualatin Mountains, likely via the route that became Springville Road (now a Forest Park trail). On reaching the Willamette, they'd raft across, trek across the St. Johns peninsula, and raft across the Columbia River. Their journey ended at Fort Vancouver where they sold the pelts to the Hudson's Bay Company. The furs were shipped to England, where they became beaver hats, a fashion accessory that had a 300-year run, ending around 1850.

3 **Once across the St. Johns Bridge, turn right on Bridge Avenue.** Built in 1930 to connect the bridge's western end to Hwy 30, the avenue cut across the lower curves of Springville Road, which once led to the ferry landing. Cross over a creek ravine; the home on the left, 8776, was built in 1913. It predates Bridge Avenue, and would have had a Springville Road address. Next to it, but deep in the ravine below Bridge Avenue, is its neighbor at 8766, also originally on Springville. Once the avenue was built and separated them, the only way to get from one house to the other is a set of 70 stairs. Descend the stairs if you are a fan of Portland's nooks. They end near the lower house. Though it has a Bridge Avenue address, it can only be accessed via Hwy 30.

These stairs allowed residents of the few streets above where you're standing to catch the United Railways passenger train that ran between downtown Portland and Banks. The line also carried freight. Passenger service ended in the 1930s, not long after the stairs were built.

On Bridge Avenue, pass Springville and Germantown Roads. Notice the beautiful rockwork at Springville and Bridge Avenue. It was one of thousands of WPA projects across the nation that created meaningful infrastructure work during the Great Depression. These two roads are some of Portland's oldest roads, likely improvements made to game or Native American trails across the Tualatin Mountains. After the fur-trapping era, Springville Road was improved in 1843, with hopes it could become a major market road for farmers on the north end of the Tualatin Valley. And indeed, for a few decades it was used that way, with produce hauled uphill from towns like North Plains, and downhill to the road that ran into Portland. Even at its heyday, it wasn't much of a road, more of a trail.

The little community of Springville, at the bottom of Springville Road, had a hotel, warehouse and other amenities, but was pretty much gone by the early 1870s, having been superseded by the rail line into the Tualatin Valley that made shipping produce a lot easier. Today the old Springville Road is just a trail in Forest Park, where it climbs to Skyline Blvd. From there it turns back into a road, dropping into new subdivisions hatching on former agricultural lands of the Tualatin Valley.

4 Cross Bridge Avenue carefully (watch for cars turning onto it) **and walk left on a sidewalk and an elevated sidewalk along Hwy 30,** which runs 3,073 miles from Astoria, Oregon to Atlantic City, New Jersey. (The "0" in 30 is a clue that it's an east-west route. North-south routes end in "1.") Before it became part of the US highway system in 1926, it started its existence as the Portland-Sauvie Island wagon road, cut into the wilderness by settlers in 1852.

Because it's a nasty, wind-tunnelish walk here, the route pulls you off and up into the hills at every chance. On the elevated sidewalk, ignore (or investigate) a 69-step newish staircase to a townhome complex. Pass a short staircase down to Hwy 30 and then the elevated sidewalk descends to the road.

You're walking here atop the Portland Hills Fault, which extends along the base of the Tualatin Mountains from Scappoose to downtown Portland. It's considered active, with major activity within the last 15,000 to 12,000 years. This fault will not be the cause of "the Big One"—the quake that'll change everything. That quake will be triggered by movement at the Cascadia Subduction Zone, about 50 miles off the Oregon Coast.

At Harbor Blvd, turn left and hairpin up the hill for instant relief from Hwy 30's racket and wind. Ignore or investigate dead-end Hardy and follow Harbor west. Stop at Roseway. Roseway and the streets that cling to the hillside above it are wonderfully interesting to explore; this is one of Linnton's micro neighborhoods. I recommend a meander up Harbor to explore Rosaria and Elva, both parallel to Roseway, and all ending in steep, uncrossable ravines. The are some of the city's remotest streets, with a surprisingly eclectic line up of homes, dating from Linnton's early days to recent. Views are wonderful. Beyond St. Johns' industrial waterfront you can see a big clump of dark green trees. That's Pier Park, in the far corner of St. Johns.

Back at the Harbor/Roseway intersection, veer right onto Roseway. An optional staircase is at 9450: if you want more steps, descend its 80 wooden steps, then come back up. The strip of land to the left as you descend is owned by the Bureau of Environmental Services. It's a creek, wildly choked by invasive holly, bamboo, and ivy. A little neighborly love and it could be a spectacular cascade during the wet season.

Just beyond the garage at 9663, descend a metal staircase to an elevated sidewalk and turn left. Walk briefly along the highway. On your left is another newish, metal staircase. Why it's there, I don't know; it leads to a sketchy little trail at the dead-end of Roseway, a street that has two perfectly good staircases. Want to climb it? It's 44 steps, each way.

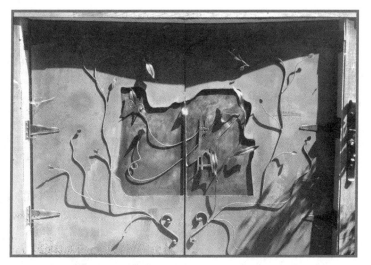

A Linnton garage door

At the top of Linnton Hill, a remnant of one of the many small farms that once existed in the Tualatin Mountains

Turn left onto Hoge, which starts in a creek valley. Walk the asphalt path on the right and encounter a street that feels like a curbless, sidewalk-free outpost of the tidy Rose City Park neighborhood. The grand home at 9940 was built in 1912, back when Linnton was a timber town separate from Portland, and before its waterfront began transitioning into a fuel storage and shipping center.

5 **At the X-shaped intersection, investigate streets above.** If you do, look for a half-overgrown empty reservoir on Mackay; it's from before 1913, when Linnton started getting Bull Run water.

Or to stay on the stair walk route, keep far right, onto Wilark (named for Linnton's Clark and Wilson Lumber Company). Just past the last home/garage, descend a staircase to an elevated sidewalk. Turn left on Hwy 30. Pass a bus stop and hiking trailhead at Linnton Creek, which runs bountifully in winter and spring. The Linnton Trail here runs into Forest Park, connecting with many trails. The pooping dog sculpture (it's a bag dispenser!) at the trailhead, along with other Linnton street art, is by sculptor and Linnton resident Ivan McLean. You can see his sculptures atop entrances to many New Seasons Markets.

If the creek is running, take a stroll out and back on the Linnton Trail, just to see what's in the woods. Forest Park is at its prettiest when it's super wet, and the ferns are ebulliently erect.

6 **On Hwy 30, watch for another staircase. Climb it.** This is a good one: 106 stairs up to the old Linnton grade school. The school closed in 1971 and it's now Linnton School Place condominiums. Linnton kids now bus to Skyline Elementary School, far out in the West Hills, and then bus to downtown's Lincoln High School.

At the top of the stairs, walk right and you'll be at the end of 2nd Street, on Linnton Hill, the main Linnton neighborhood. (The numbered streets in Linnton, unlike the rest of Portland, are not "avenues." This is a relic of Linnton's days as an independent town.)

Two big homes on the right were built in the 1910s by the Clark and the Wilson families, owners of the Clark and Wilson Lumber Company mill. From their windows, the owners could look down on the workings of the mill. Mill workers lived on the streets around the executives, in an era nothing like today, when the average CEO pays himself 270 times the amount he pays the average worker. They're not living in the same neighborhoods anymore.

Linnton is connected to one of Portland's great philanthropists, Maybelle Clark Macdonald (1916-2009). Her father Wilson Clark and grandfather Orange Clark started Clark and Wilson Lumber Company in 1905, with relatives John and Charles Wilson. Wilson Clark and his family lived in Linnton until 1915, when they moved into the Nob Hill neighborhood. Maybelle was born there.

The Clarks also owned vast timberlands. Their timber wealth has been shared since 1970 via the Maybelle Clark Macdonald Foundation. It has contributed millions to support and expand programs at Oregon schools and arts organizations, and to help Oregonians suffering from poverty, hunger, abuse, or dependencies.

Maybelle's older brother Maurie Clark, who was born in Linnton, co-created with Gordon Smith the famous Camp 18 logging museum/restaurant on the Sunset Highway in the 1970s.

After 1948, the Clark and Wilson mill became the Linnton Plywood Mill. It closed in 2001 and was demolished in 2017. Plans are to restore the site to off-channel, salmon-friendly habitat.

To stay on the hill and investigate the streets above and beyond this point, see below. Or to end the walk now, walk out 2nd and veer left on 3rd Court, following it to 3rd Street and the top of 176 stairs. Descend to Hwy 30. Across the highway is this walk's reward, lunch and a beer at The Lighthouse Restaurant and Bar, in an 1886 building that has been a bank, barber shop, and post office. The restaurant's been there since 1950, with new owners in 2016.

Catch the bus at 107th and Hwy 30, where you can learn a bit more Linnton history and enjoy "Ma Olsen's Garden." It sits where Nora Olsen's grocery was, before a 1960s road widening razed it and all the businesses on this side of the highway. In the 2010s the blackberry-choked site was replanted with native plants by neighbors, for your enjoyment. They were inspired by a San Francisco garden created by a citizen atop a former garbage dump along the Filbert Steps.

If you love exploring hilly streets and dead-ends, explore the roads on the map before you descend to your beer. Things to look for:

- 5th Street, at the top of Linnton's street grid. A 12-acre farm, with old Oregon white oaks, was sold to Portland Parks & Recreation in 2017, extending the acreage of Forest Park a bit. The City buys undeveloped land adjacent to Forest Park to prevent development and reduce fire risks, an annual worry each summer and fall.

- The 108th and 109th staircases (92 and 57 stairs, respectively). They used to connect to Hwy 30 before it was widened.

- A Portland water tank, with a bootleg path into the woods behind it

- A metal garage with a rendition of the St. Johns Bridge welded to it

STAIRS, IN ORDER ENCOUNTERED	UP OR DOWN	NUMBER
1. Cathedral Park, under the St. Johns Bridge	Up	41
2. Bridge Avenue to near Hwy 30	Both	140*
3. Hwy 30 to townhome complex	Both	138*
4. Roseway at 9450 to Hwy 30	Both	160*
5. Roseway at 9663 to Hwy 30	Down	67
6. Hoge at Hwy 30 to path at Roseway dead–end	Both	88*
7. Wilark to Hwy 30	Down	42
8. Hwy 30 to 2nd Street	Up	106
9. 3rd Court to Hwy 30	Down	176
10. 108th between 2nd and 3rd streets	Both	184*
11. 109th between 2nd and 3rd streets	Both	114*
Total on route		**432**
*Nearby optional stairs, both up and down		**1,256**

Alameda Ridge

T HIS 6.5-MILE WALK IS A STAIRCASE-TREASURE HUNT THROUGH THE diagonals, curves, and hidden streets of Alameda Ridge. The intricate maneuvering to find all 11 flights of stairs happens in the walk's first half. With many short ups and downs via the staircases, the route gains and loses a total of about 500 feet in elevation.

The stair walk's midpoint offers food options along Sandy Boulevard. From there, you can put the book away. It's a linear cruise in the flats back to the start. Use the map, or meander back on any combination of streets; they're all worth exploring.

ALAMEDA CAT

A SIDEWALK BETWEEN HOMES LEADS TO WEST HILLS VIEWS AND A STAIRCASE

OLD AND NEW HOMES ON ALAMEDA RIDGE

Neighborhoods

SABIN, ALAMEDA, BEAUMONT-WILSHIRE, ROSE CITY PARK, HOLLYWOOD, GRANT PARK, IRVINGTON

CULLY

ROSE CITY PARK

ROSE CITY CEMETERY

52ND AVE
51ST AVE
50TH AVE

50TH AVE
49TH AVE

SANDY BLVD

6

47TH AVE

KLICKITAT ST

SISKIYOU ST

STANTON ST

ALAMEDA ST

WISTARIA DR

BRAZEE ST

THOMPSON ST

TILLAMOOK ST

BEAUMONT

WILSHIRE

SHAVER ST

BEECH ST

44TH AVE

42ND AVE

41ST AVE

43RD AVE

42ND AVE

FREMONT ST

FAILING ST

Wilshire Park

37TH AVE

35TH AVE

ALAMEDA ST

4

5

STANTON ST

CÉSAR E CHÁVEZ BLVD

38TH AVE

36TH AVE

35TH AVE

MORRIS ST

36TH AVE
35TH PL
35TH AVE

MALTBY

Barnes Mansion

ALAMEDA ST

3

32ND PL

BRYCE ST

DUNCKLEY ST

HAMBLET ST

ALAMEDA ST

STUART

EDGEHILL PL

ALAMEDA TERRE

Autzen Mansion

GILE

RIDGEWOOD DR

2

REGENTS DR

FREMONT ST

33RD A

32ND A

ALAMEDA

ALAMEDA ELEMENTARY SCHOOL

KLICKITAT ST

STANTON ST

SISKIYOU ST

26TH AVE

24TH AVE

23RD AVE

21ST AVE

19TH AVE

17TH AVE

KNOTT ST

GRANT PARK

Grant Park

Beverly Cleary Sculpture Garden

GRANT HIGH SCHOOL

7

BRAZEE ST

THOMPSON ST

TILLAMOOK ST

US GRANT PL

28TH AVE

IRVINGTON

HOLLYWOOD

HOLLYWOOD LIBRARY

SABIN

Sabin Hydro Park

1

SHAVER ST

PRESCOTT ST

SKIDMORE ST

MASON ST

22ND AVE

29TH AVE

28TH AVE

N

MAP SCALE

0 MILES   1/8

Directions: The Quick Guide

1 ▪▪▪ Begin at the Sabin HydroPark and Community Garden, 1907 NE Skidmore Street.

▪▪▪ Walk south on 19th, and in one block descend 51 stairs. Walk straight for a block.

▪▪▪ Turn left onto Alameda. At 22nd, turn right on Gile Terrace, then right on Alameda.

▪▪▪ At 26th (on left) and Stuart Drive (on right), turn right on Stuart; immediately look right for the staircase. Descend 75 stairs to Ridgewood and turn left.

2 ▪▪▪ Pass 25th (on right). At a wide intersection, turn left on Stuart. Past the first house are 70 stairs. Climb, then turn right on Alameda.

▪▪▪ At 29th, Regents, Alameda, and on the right, Alameda Terrace, turn right on Alameda Terrace.

▪▪▪ At 3130, descend to Fremont and turn left.

▪▪▪ Just before 32nd, climb 65 stairs to Alameda Terrace and turn right.

▪▪▪ At Alameda Terrace, Alameda and 32nd Place, turn right on Alameda.

3 ▪▪▪ Turn right on 33rd. Cross Fremont; continue south on 33rd one block.

▪▪▪ At Klickitat, cross 33rd at the crosswalk. Walk uphill on Klickitat.

▪▪▪ Turn left on 35th, then right on Fremont.

▪▪▪ Turn right on 35th Place, then left on Maltby.

▪▪▪ Turn left on 36th, and walk to Fremont.

4 ■ ■ Walk one block east on Fremont and turn right on Alameda.

■ ■ Descend stairs just past 3868 to 38th Avenue and turn left.

■ ■ Turn left on Wistaria. Cross to walk its south side.

■ ■ Avoid a blind crossing of high-speed 41st: from Wistaria, curve right onto Cesar Chavez Blvd, then left on Stanton. Turn left on 42nd and walk one block to Wistaria.

5 ■ ■ Cross Wistaria to a staircase east of 4131. Climb to Alameda and turn right.

■ ■ Past 4420, turn right on a sidewalk to a staircase. Descend to Wistaria at 43rd and turn left.

■ ■ Keep left on Wistaria where it splits with 43rd.

■ ■ Not far past 48th, descend stairs to 49th's dead-end. Walk out 49th and turn left on Brazee.

■ ■ Turn left on 50th. Climb 43 stairs to lower Wistaria and turn right.

■ ■ Continue right where upper Wistaria comes in.

■ ■ At Alameda, turn hard right onto Wistaria again.

■ ■ Beyond 5126 descend 50 stairs to 51st Ave. Walk one block to Sandy Blvd's food and drink options.

6 ■ ■ From 51st, turn right on Sandy Blvd.

■ ■ Just past 49th, veer right onto Thompson.

■ ■ At 36th, turn right to walk around Grant High, through Grant Park.

■ ■ Exit the park at 33rd and Brazee and walk west on Brazee.

7 ■ ■ At 26th and Brazee, enter historic Irvington.

■ ■ Turn right on 19th, which leads back to the start.

The Big Flood

Unlike most of Portland's volcanic hills, Alameda Ridge is a 6-mile hill of gravels, sand, and cobbles deposited by the Missoula Floods of the last Ice Age—18,000 to 15,000 years ago. Repeated breaching of ice dams on Glacial Lake Missoula in today's western Montana resulted in titanic floods that roared westward, following the Columbia River.

Geologists believe they were perhaps the earth's most cataclysmic floods. When they erupted out of the tight confines of the Columbia River Gorge they hit Portland like a mega tsunami: water almost 400 feet deep inundated all of North and Northeast Portland except the top 200 feet of Rocky Butte. Geologists believe approximately 40 floods took place over 3,000 years.

Waters flowed as far south as Eugene—100 miles from Portland—then reversed, flowing through the Portland Basin again as they drained back out to the Columbia. All that churn left a lot of debris on the landscape. The deep, plush soils of the Willamette Valley arrived via the floods, and rocks (called glacial erratics since they are not of local origin) surfed here, embedded in the ice. Many of these erratics were large chunks of granite (and even a meteorite in one case), that have been carted off, carved up, or used as monuments, but plenty still exist, for rock hounds to find.

Alameda Ridge is one of several pendant bars the floods deposited in the Portland area. This type of gravel bar is found downstream of an erosion-resistant protrusion such as a large outcrop of bedrock (Rocky Butte, in Alameda Ridge's case). Another pendant bar is in Troutdale, the ridge running southwest from Broughton Bluff, which is the westernmost cliff of the Columbia River Gorge.

In the early 1900s, Alameda Ridge was mined for sand and gravel. It was called Gravelly Hill, and a quarry operated at 33rd and Fremont. The name "Alameda" was the brainchild of a real estate developer in the early 1900s. Once high-value view lots began being sold, the ridge's gravel-mining days were left behind.

1 **Begin at 19th and Skidmore, at the Sabin HydroPark.** Portland's seven HydroParks are hilly sites where Portland Water Bureau's tanks or towers are set among enough greenspace to become a de facto park. Most HydroParks used to be fenced off for security reasons, which, upon scrutiny by a skeptical public, didn't really merit a fence. So the fences came down and new parks were born.

Portland's water comes primarily from the 102-square mile Bull Run Watershed, a pristine and highly protected forest 26 miles east of Portland. From Bull Run Lake, at 3,300 feet elevation, water flows downhill into two reservoirs. After the water's been treated with chlorine to disinfect it and sodium hydroxide to raise its pH (to avoid corroding copper and lead in pipes of homes and businesses) it flows via gravity into underground storage tanks on Kelly and Powell buttes. From there it flows to end users or to the many towers or tanks scattered all over Portland's higher elevations and then downhill into homes and businesses.

Fun fact: In summer, the 935,000 Bull Run customers consume 120 to 160 million gallons per day. In winter, that drops to 80 million gallons per day.

Walk south on 19th past beautifully recharged 1940s and 50s bungalows and a nice city view. At the dead-end, descend the westernmost of the ridge's 11 staircases. At the bottom, meander around the Sabin Community Orchard. Good signage offers up tidbits like "There are 7,000 varieties of apples grown in the world."

In one block, turn left onto Alameda. (Note: Alameda becomes Shaver Street west of 19th.) At 22nd, turn right on Gile Terrace, a two-block-long lane one realtor called "Portland's most European street." You're now in the Alameda neighborhood, where English Tudor style is everywhere. Look for half-timbering (i.e., structural wooden members exposed on the façade), second-story overhangs, steeply-pitched roofs with gables facing the street, an asymmetric composition, and facades of brick combined with stucco.

Walk Gile's length. Where it rejoins Alameda, turn right. Before you walk on, look across Alameda to a large home. It's the Autzen Mansion, a Tudor beauty built in 1926 for Thomas J. Autzen (1888-1958). He made millions in the family business, Portland Manufacturing Company. When Thomas was 17 in 1905, his dad sent him to the Portland's World's Fair to show manufacturers a new product: a three-ply plywood made of Douglas fir. Demand exploded and the company's fortunes were made. In the early 1950s, Autzen and his son Thomas E. created the Autzen Foundation. Its large gift to the University of Oregon in the 1960s helped build Autzen Stadium, home of the Ducks.

Two Portland Heritage trees are on the property. On the left is a European copper beech (*Fagus sylvatica* f. *purpurea)*, a grand tree that needs a big property to grow on. Rising behind the house you can see the canopy of a canyon live oak (*Quercus chrysolepis)*. It's an evergreen oak native to California and far southwest Oregon.

On Alameda at 26th (on left) and Stuart Drive (on right), turn right on Stuart; immediately look right for the staircase. Hang on to the railing—narrow treads here! Descend 75 stairs to Ridgewood Drive and turn left. Thank you, anonymous donor, for the bench midway, so walkers can spend some time in stillness, enjoying these exceptionally pretty stairs.

2 **Walk past 25th (on right). At a wide intersection, turn hard left on Stuart. On the right is a staircase, past the first house. Climb to Alameda Street and turn right.** This long, straight-as-an-arrow staircase is one of the prettiest on the walk, with sword fern, euphorbia, hypericum, and vinca framing its margins.

On Alameda, cross 29th, then Regents, and turn right on Alameda Terrace. Like Gile Terrace, Alameda Terrace is another short half-moon lane carved onto the ridge's south slope. At 3130, descend to Fremont and turn left.

Just before 32nd, climb 65 stairs back to Alameda Terrace, and turn right. At Alameda Terrace, Alameda and NE 32nd Place, turn right on Alameda. Home styles are more varied: Dutch Colonial, midcentury ranches, and a more stripped down version of Arts and Crafts and Colonial styles, reflecting a Modernist sensibility.

❸ Turn right on 33rd. Cross Fremont at the light and continue south on 33rd. Beverly Cleary, Oregon's most famous author, grew up nearby. In her autobiography she writes of sledding this hill in the 1920s (then known as 33rd Street). In her Portland-based children's books, Henry Huggins and Ramona Quimby lived on Klickitat Street. Cleary herself lived on Tillamook east of 33rd as a grade-schooler, and on 37th south of Morris as a teenager. (See *Walking with Ramona; Exploring Beverly Cleary's Portland* for more about this neighborhood in the 1920s and 30s.)

One of the ridge's gravel quarries was at 33rd and Fremont, and was later filled with construction, garbage and other debris, a common practice. Uneven settlement of the fill has resulted in some nearby houses dealing with skewed foundations. Here you can see upheaved sidewalks and deformed asphalt on 33rd, evidence of settling soils.

At Klickitat, cross 33rd at the pedestrian crosswalk. Walk uphill on Klickitat. You're in the Beaumont-Wilshire neighborhood now. Pass charming storybook-like homes on the right and massive retaining walls on the left, including some impressive backyard terraces made with recycled concrete sidewalks.

At 3533 is a 32-room home on eight city lots. The Barnes Mansion was built in 1914 by Frank C. and Isabella Barnes in a subdivision/family compound they created and called "Irene Heights" after one of their seven children. Barnes came to Oregon in 1861 as a seven-year-old. His father William Barnes became Portland's road supervisor, and oversaw the opening of a county road to the Tualatin Valley, which was named in his honor: Barnes Road. Frank's early days farming beaver dam land in today's Beaverton led to a meat market at SW 3rd and Morrison, as well as a salmon cannery. And to wealth.

Take a detour to look at the homes built for the Barnes' children in the compound-turned-neighborhood.

After regarding the front of the home, go back to 35th and walk north on it. Behind the mansion, at 3424 NE 35th, is a gorgeous Prairie style home built for the family in 1911, a few years before the mansion was built. They moved here from Irvington. Deep eaves and a horizontal aspect are hallmarks of that style, made famous in the Midwest by architects such as Frank Lloyd Wright. It occupies three city lots. It became daughter Gladys's home, with husband John Reynolds, who like all of Barnes's six sons-in-law, worked for the family business.

From 35th, turn right on Fremont. The home at 3526 was home to daughter Irene Barnes Hendrickson. It's more modest than Gladys's home, but has two eyebrow dormers, which enhance its cuteness factor. And it sits on three lots, not bad.

From Fremont, turn right on 35th Place, which ends at Maltby. Turn left. In the right corner sits the lovely garage for the Barnes Mansion. The Colonial Revival at 3601 was built for daughter Lila Barnes Starr at the same time the mansion was built. It sits on four lots.

Follow Maltby as it bends and becomes 36th. The home at 3414 is a Dutch Colonial built for son Frank S. in 1916, at age 27. He didn't live here much, as he managed the family's Alaska salmon canning operations. Frank died after being mauled by a grizzly bear in Alaska. The last house, at the corner of Fremont and 36th (3460 NE 36th) is another Dutch Colonial, built for daughter Clara Barnes Collinson in 1916.

4 From 36th, turn right on Fremont and right on Alameda. Once you cross Klickitat you're back in big-view territory. I have always loved the tile scene in the front façade of a Spanish Colonial at 3810; find another one at 3828.

Just past 3868, descend stairs to 38th and turn left. Turn left on Wistaria and cross to walk its downhill side. The next few turns avoid a blind crossing of fast, curvy 41st/42nd: from Wistaria, curve south onto Cesar Chavez Blvd, then turn left on Stanton. Cross 42nd at the painted crosswalk and turn left. Walk one block to Wistaria.

5 At 42nd and Wistaria, cross Wistaria to a staircase at the stop sign. Climb 127 stairs—the longest on the route-- to Alameda and turn right. Pass impeccably landscaped homes and turn right past 4420 to a staircase. Descend 118 stairs to Wistaria at 43rd and turn left, keeping on Wistaria where it splits east and 43rd goes south. If you want to stay up on Alameda, where more huge homes line the ridge top, climb back up the 118-step staircase (or skip it if you don't mind not completing the whole 11-staircase circuit), and walk Alameda to 48th. Descend this lovely little block and jump back into the directions at 48th and Wistaria.

On Wistaria, walk to 48th. Homes on Wistaria here have river-rock retaining walls. The rock is likely deposited by the Missoula Floods, quarried from the ridge.

Not far past 48th, descend 30 stairs to 49th and a lower level of Wistaria. Walk straight (south) on 49th to Brazee and turn left, then left on 50th. This is one of the city's most wonderful blocks: a dead-end lined with gorgeous Craftsman bungalows, with a staircase at the end.

At 50th's dead-end, climb 43 stairs to Lower Wistaria; turn right. Continue right where upper Wistaria comes in. At Alameda, turn hard right onto Wistaria again. At 5126, descend the last of

Alameda Ridge's 11 staircases to 51st. Walk out to Sandy Blvd, with food options, left and right.

6 At 51st, turn right on Sandy Blvd, one of Portland's most historic roads. Oregon Trail pioneers walked this route from the mouth of the Sandy River, where they'd landed after a harrowing passage on the wind-whipped, whitewater-pocked Columbia River from Dalles City (now The Dalles). Before them, the path had been made by Native Americans, traveling between the Sandy River and Willamette Falls, an ancient fishing and trading site in Oregon City.

Just past 49th, veer right off Sandy onto Thompson. At 36th, go right to walk around newly renovated Grant High, then west through Grant Park; exit the park at 33rd and Brazee. Just before you leave the park are sculptures of Beverly Cleary's three most beloved characters: Ramona Quimby in her hand-me-down raincoat, Henry Huggins with the jacket he once hid kittens in during a job interview (to be a paperboy), and Ribsy whose shiny back is just right for toddlers to ride. This was Cleary's childhood park, neighborhood, and high school.

Walk west on Brazee through the Grant Park neighborhood.

7 At 26th, enter Irvington, an entire neighborhood listed on the National Register of Historic Places. Turn right on 19th and follow it into the Sabin neighborhood, and back to the start.

Passersby,
Don't be shy;
Have a sit,
Rest a bit!

A HOSPITABLE CORNER IN IRENE
HEIGHTS ON ALAMEDA RIDGE

Stairs, in order encountered	Up or Down	Number
1. Crane to Mason, on 19th	Down	51
2. Stuart to Ridgewood	Down	75
3. Stuart to Alameda	Up	70
4. Alameda Terrace to Fremont	Down	98
5. Fremont to Alameda Terrace	Up	65
6. Alameda to 38th	Down	78
7. Wistaria to Alameda	Up	127
8. Alameda to Wistaria	Down	118
9. Wistaria to 49th	Down	30
10. 50th to Wistaria	Up	43
11. Wistaria to 51	Down	83
Total on route		**838**

First Thurman St. Bridge pre-1905 with pioneer era shacks in Balch Creek gulch

Slabtown, Nob Hill, and Westover Terraces

Save this 6-mile stair walk for a clear day, to enjoy the four-mountain views. With all the climbing, it's a good cold-day hike. The route starts and ends in once blue-collar Slabtown, rises into the Arts and Crafts enclave of Willamette Heights, climbs further into well-manicured Westover Terraces, drops into the posh reaches of Nob Hill, and ends at a swath of restaurants and commerce in Slabtown.

On the route are 17 staircases, two hidden paths, and a bridge over a deep canyon. It also has fantastic near-mansions, early and ornate apartment buildings, tiny cottages, and historic streetcar business districts that are well spaced for cups of coffee and such.

The loop gains and loses about 1,000 feet.

STAIRS TO CORNELL ROAD FROM NORTHRUP STREET

DIRECTIONS: THE QUICK GUIDE

1 ▪▪ Begin at NW 29th Avenue and Wilson Street and walk one block west on Wilson.

▪▪ Turn left on 30th; walk one block, to Vaughn's dead-end at a hill. Climb 32 stairs, and go right on the uphill path to upper Vaughn. Turn left on 32nd, then right on Thurman.

▪▪ At 3424, climb 101 stairs to Aspen.

2 ▪▪ Turn left onto Aspen, then left again on Savier.

▪▪ Turn right on 33rd, and left on Quimby, continuing left as Quimby turns into 32nd.

▪▪ From 32nd, turn right on Thurman, cross the bridge and come to 29th.

3 ▪▪ Turn right on 29th. At its dead-end at Quimby, go left to a path and staircase. Climb to Cornell Road and turn left.

▪▪ Across from 2815, climb 73 stairs to Summit. Turn left, then climb 157 stairs to Westover Road.

▪▪ Turn right and walk to Westover, Cumberland, and Fairfax Terrace. Climb 131 stairs that begin at Fairfax.

4 ▪▪ At the top of the stairs, Cumberland, turn right.

▪▪ Pass Shenandoah Terrace, turn right on Luray Terrace, and climb 52 stairs to Luray Circus.

▪▪ Walk out of Luray Circus, turn right on Luray Terrace, left on Cumberland, right on Westover.

5 ▪▪ Turn left on Summit.

▪▪ Descend 33 stairs to Lovejoy; turn right on Cornell and right on 25th Place. Climb 41 stairs to Westover and turn left.

- At Westover, 25th, and Johnson, keep far right to stay on Westover. Ignore stairs on your left (at Irving).

6 - Descend 51 stairs to Glisan. Walk east to 23rd, and turn left.

- Turn left on Irving, climb 48 stairs to Westover and turn right.

- Veer right onto 25th.

7 - Turn left on Marshall to its dead-end. Climb 55 stairs to Cornell and turn right.

- Descend 63 stairs to Northrup, walk straight, then left on 25th and left on Overton.

- Climb 56 stairs to Cornell, turn right and descend 65 stairs to Pettygrove. Walk straight.

8 - Enter Wallace Park and cross through it to 25th and Raleigh.

- Turn right on Raleigh and left on 24th to Thurman.

- Eat or drink along Thurman or 23rd.

9 - On 24th north of Thurman, walk past one building. Turn left on a walkway to 24th Place. Walk out 24th Place, then left on Vaughn, left on 25th, right on Upshur, and right on 29th to the start.

The Geology Under Your Feet

On this route, flat areas are on the floor of the Portland Basin, which is layered with sands and gravels deposited over millennia by the Columbia and Willamette rivers, along with soils eroded from the Tualatin Mountains (also called the West Hills).

Public staircases lift you off the floor onto the lower flanks of the West Hills. The hills began millions of years ago as volcanic flood-basalt flows that came oozing westward from ground cracks in Eastern Oregon. The flows hardened. And then they got uplifted. Like Coyote Wall in the Columbia Gorge, the West Hills are an anticline. Faults underlying the basalt layers are pushing the layers up, just as a throw rug pushed on both sides will rise up in ripples. The West Hills are still moving.

One more element in the West Hills' birth narrative is a blanket of unstable silt blown in (called loess) from the Columbia River's floodplains in eastern Washington. That silt, called the Portland Hills Silt, is extremely slippery when it gets saturated with winter's rains. Its tendency to slide at the point of contact with the underlying basalt is the cause of many of the landslides that pockmark the face of the West Hills. Many of these historic slides, unknown when neighborhoods were developed, were discovered after the creation of high-resolution maps using LIDAR.

Relevant to one neighborhood on this route are flood deposits called the Troutdale Formation. These rounded river rocks were deposited here millions of years ago by the Columbia River—long before the Missoula Floods added their deposits to the Portland Basin. Westover Terraces is a human-terraced neighborhood created when a water cannon blasted these river rocks off the face of the hills and down toward the Willamette River.

1 Begin at NW 29th Avenue and Wilson Street. Walk one block west on Wilson. About a block on the right is the boundary of the 1,600-acre Guild's Lake Industrial Sanctuary. It's a sanctuary because it's been reserved by the City of Portland for manufacturing, distribution and other industrial activities. No residential, mixed use, or large retail is allowed to move in and clog up roads with cars and wayward pedestrians. The goal: high-paying jobs and efficient industrial infrastructure close to where people live. (By the way, *Guild* rhymes with *file*, not *build*.)

Guild's Lake used to be a real lake. Before the Willamette was channeled into its present canal-like tube, it widened into shallow lakes and marshes during the wet season. Here, you would've been standing a few hundred feet from the shore of Guild's Lake, named for Peter and Eliza Guild, who settled on its shores. As early as the 1880s, the lakebed began to be filled with material sluiced off the hillside and dredge spoils from the river. By the 1920s it had been totally filled, ready for industrial use. Then came the Depression, when not much happened. In World War II, temporary housing was constructed at the still mostly vacant new land at Guild's Lake. Ten thousand people lived here during the war. All that housing was later torn down.

Stop for a moment at Wilson and 30th. The home at the corner, at 3007, is one of the city's oldest, dating from 1874. Originally, it sat a few blocks west, on the road to Astoria that ran along Guild's Lake (today's St. Helens Road).

The glass and concrete building behind you is Montgomery Park. It was built in 1922 as a Montgomery Ward store and distribution center. Ward's used to be an iconic American retailer, like Sears or J.C. Penney. In 1976 the warehouse closed, and in 1986 redeveloper Bill Naito bought the building and turned it into an event and conference center with offices. Its famous neon sign—the city's largest--needed only two letters changed during the renovation, turning "Ward" into "Park," a wonderfully economical bit of adaptive reuse.

Turn left on 30th and walk to a remote block of Vaughn. At its dead-end, climb 32 stairs, then go right on a short, uphill path to an even more remote section of Vaughn. The path, which I count as one of the two hidden paths in this route, ends at a little-traveled warren of streets that I recommend going off-route to explore. Here you're in the lower flanks of Willamette Heights, in an area bypassed by people heading into the Heights on their way to Forest Park.

Pass two spectacular chimneys on the right: one river rock and one clinker brick. Clinker bricks—the misshapen, often glassified brick that got too hot in the kiln—used to be discarded. In the Arts and Crafts design movement of the 1800s, its organic forms were celebrated and pulled from the refuse heap. You'll see it all over town, but this is an especially exuberant use of it.

Turn left on 32nd, then right on Thurman. Take your time here. Thurman Street, once home to Ursula K. LeGuin, is an uphill runway of beautiful big Arts and Crafts homes, culminating at a popular entrance into Forest Park, the Leif Erikson Trail. Except for Linnton, this is the city's most remote neighborhood. It is bounded on one side by Balch Creek's steep canyon; on another by Guild's Lake, and on the other two sides, its streets lap up against slopes of wilderness.

2 Cross Thurman at 34th. At 3424, climb 101 stairs to Aspen and turn left. More wonderful homes here, at the top of Willamette Heights. See the map for Forest Park trailheads accessible from here. Come back for a hike on another day.

Turn left on Savier. Most homes in Willamette Heights date from the early 1900s. The six giant homes lining up here on the right are a century younger. Behind them the hill rises 100 feet, a nob once called Scotch Nubbin. In 1907 an entrepreneur began sluicing this nubbin away, leaving behind a precipitous cliff.

Turn right on 33rd, heading downhill toward Balch Creek's canyon. 33rd ends at Quimby, which runs along the top of the canyon wall. At 33rd and Quimby, walk to the right (it looks like a private road, but the street right-of-way extends to the far edge of the house). You're looking at one incredible home, the Hoke House. It was designed by Portland's Skylab Architecture with an outrageous cantilever that minimizes its footprint and carries the living space right into the face of nature. Photos on Skylab's site let you see more of this masterpiece.

From 33rd and Quimby, turn left on Quimby, which curves into 32nd. This street is a parade of great old wood-shingled homes and epic personal staircases. Willamette Heights is where the city first saw the Arts and Crafts style, and just about every home is a wonderful blend of original architecture and owner creativity.

From 32nd, turn right on Thurman. Walk a block and look up at the big white house on the right. It dates from 1892, two years after the neighborhood was platted out, when someone built a grand home atop a rise overlooking Guild's Lake.

Past 31st, the swell Thurman Street Bridge begins. Give a nod to the pinecone finial at the approach, then stop midway for a look and some stories about what you're seeing here. Originally called the Balch Gulch Bridge, it's Oregon's oldest bridge, from 1905. Structural repairs in 2014 replaced all of its components above the deck truss, including the wooden sidewalks (now steel, with ridges to chew up leaves, and holes for water to drain). The chain link railing that had been an "improvement" in the 1950s is gone, and new railing, modeled after the original design, is now in place.

On a clear day you can see four Cascade volcanoes, left to right: Mt. Rainier, peaking over Mt. St. Helens' left shoulder, then Mt. Adams, then Mt. Hood, dead-ahead. Below is the canyon of Balch Creek, where in the 1850s Danford (aka Danforth) and Mary Jane Balch eked out a living in the gloom of old growth forest. Danford became enraged when their teenage daughter Anna eloped to marry the wonderfully-named Mortimer Stump. Shortly after the marriage, Balch, who had an alcohol problem, encountered the newlyweds at the Stark Street Ferry, and shot his new son-in-law to death. He claimed it was accidental. Balch escaped custody for a time, living in the woods above the canyon until he was caught and ultimately hanged. The execution, in 1859, took place at the site of today's Salmon Street Springs.

Balch Creek is one of the Tualatin Mountains' bigger creeks, rumbling noisily in winter and spring, and meekly stair-stepping downhill in summer and fall. Just beyond the wooden trash rack that catches tree limbs and debris, the creek gets fed into a pipe. It once flowed freely into Guild's Lake itself, but now a pipe carries it through landfill to where it dumps into the Willamette. The artificially flat ground below the bridge is part of that landfill, which occurred around 1910.

Also below is where Forest Park's first headquarters was established in 1948 when the park was cobbled together from various land parcels, many owned by folks who cut the timber, then ditched paying taxes on the now-worthless land. Their delinquency became a gift to the rest of us: a 5,000-acre wilderness park. The area below the bridge is one of the park's main portals, accessed by car or bike via Upshur Street. A particularly historic and wonderful trail, the Macleay Trail, starts here and follows Balch Creek into deep woods, connecting with other Forest Park trails.

Investigate the below-the-bridge landscape, if you want, by taking 71 stairs down. They're not on the route, but there's a restroom down there, plus it's interesting to look up from below the bridge. The stairs descend from the northeast end of the bridge. Cross Thurman carefully if you take them: for a dead-end, it's very busy.

3 **After the Thurman Street Bridge, turn right on 29th, a San Francisco-steep street.** At 1625 look up at a nice old Colonial Revival. It was built in 1893 by Harry Clarke. At age 23, in 1888, he

SUMMIT AVENUE TO WESTOVER ROAD MEGA STAIRCASE

became president of the company his dad founded, Portland Iron Works. Harry built this house when he was 29. He could leave the front door, pick up the streetcar on Savier, and be down to his Slabtown factory in a minute. Portland Iron Works made industrial saws, engines, and other parts for the timber industry on Northrup, between 13th and 14th.

At 29th's dead-end, slip beyond the sidewalk to a stub of Quimby. On the left, find a path to 25 stairs up to Cornell Road. At the top, turn left. William Cornell improved this road in the 1850s. He lived about where Cornell and Miller roads intersect today. In the late 1800s you'd have seen horse-drawn wagons on this road, full of produce from the Cedar Mill area. Like Canyon Road, Cornell was a market road by which produce from the Tualatin Valley was brought to docks and consumers in Portland.

The gorgeous cubes of homes on the left were built in 2013, replacing a midcentury ranch. The left one, "Tower House," has a 25-foot steel bridge connecting its third floor to the road. It's four floors, each one or two rooms, and was designed by Portland architect Benjamin Waechter. A bit further on, a private garden on Cornell provides open space for a fantastic view.

Across from 2815, on the right are 73 stairs to Summit. Carefully cross Cornell, and climb. At the top turn left. After Summit Court's intersection, look right for another, very long staircase. Climb 157 stairs to Westover Road. This is Westover Terraces, a neighborhood born of extreme violence to the land. Beginning in 1910, a machine called a hydraulic giant attacked what had been called Goldsmith's Hill, directing bolts of water that dislodged everything targeted: rocks, trees, soil, sand, gravel. The Oregonian marveled in a 1911 headline, midway through the project, "Goldsmith's Hill Melts Away." In 1914, the completed Westover Terrace project was called "one of the largest pieces of hydraulic excavation in the country" in a laudatory article by a national engineering magazine.

Turn right and walk to Westover, Cumberland Road, and Fairfax Terrace. Look for another wondrous staircase on Fairfax. Climb 131 stairs to Cumberland and turn right. The materials, carried off the hill in wooden sluices, filled part of Guild's Lake and the lower portion of Balch Creek's gulch. The Troutdale Formation gravel was not used in the landfill; it was washed and sold. Much of it was used by United Railways as ballast rock for interurban rail lines.

4 **Walk past Shenandoah Terrace, then go right on Luray Terrace. Look left and climb 52 stairs to Luray Circus.** There are no elephants or clowns here, just a circle (*circus*) with three large homes arrayed around it. The home at 3002, framed by tall Douglas firs, was designed in 1931 by Morris Whitehouse. In confirming my amateur's interpretation of this home's style, my architecture historian friend Eric Wheeler offered this snippet of enthusiastic expertise:

> "It has the English Arts and Crafts massing and details, but there is a Modernist feel to the horizontality and the distinctive convex recessed brick entry. The…use of the vertical brick detail in the lintel suggests a keystone in a very restrained manner. [It] represents a transition from the derivative Period Revivals of the 1920s to the Modernism of Post-WW II residential architecture."

Perhaps you've already noticed this: Names for the streets here, such as Culpepper, Cumberland, Albemarle, and Shenandoah, evoke the cultured gentility of old Virginia. In real estate coding that means "costs a lot."

Walk out of Luray Circus, then turn right on Luray Terrace. A vacant lot gives you a fantastic view, all the way to the St. Johns Bridge. One mile nearer is the 1912 Railroad Bridge. To the left is the green of Forest Park. The land at its base was once a series of interconnected wetland lakes: Guild's, Doan, Kittredge, that flooded and drained with the river's changing levels. The slow-moving water in those lakes offered young salmon good places to grow before heading to the Pacific. Across the Willamette, ships can be seen docked at Swan Island, some in its dry dock, where cruise ships, military ships, and others go for repairs.

Follow Luray to Cumberland, and turn left. At Cumberland, Fairfax, and Westover, turn right on Westover and cross to walk its east side. Westover is broad and offers great homes to look at, as well as homes far above on the terrace one level up. The terraces created here were designed so that each level offered great views; the Olmsted Brothers landscape architecture firm, known for its nonlinear approach to design, was hired to design the street layout. See the map; it shows streets above Cornell curving around the face of the mountain, in sharp contrast to the more linear alignment downslope.

5 **Turn left on Summit. Look for a bold, basalt-tiled slope on the left. Across are 33 stairs. Descend them to what used to be called "the head of Lovejoy Street."** Enjoy the giant sequoia at the base of the stairs. This secluded dead-end block, unknown even to longtime Portlanders, is a jackpot for urban walkers. Don't miss the red-brick home on the right at 2642. Built in 1908 in a nice mix of Craftsman and Colonial Revival, its first residents must have gritted their teeth for several years while the hillside above them was ripped apart. The house was designed by our famous A.E. Doyle, who designed Central Library among many other Portland treasures. It's the Harmon/Neils House, named for the first two families who owned it. Recent owners replaced the roof with Vermont slate.

Wander down Marcia Street (mar-see-uh) to the Modernist home at 2558. It was built in 1999 by architect Ned Vaivoda. The firm he founded with his former partner Robert Thompson, TVA Architects, designed much of the Nike campus in Beaverton. It's certainly different from the historic homes, but the scale and red brick tie it to the neighborhood pretty well, I'd say. It sold in 2015 to new owners.

Come out of Lovejoy and turn right on Cornell, then immediately right on 25th Place. Climb 41 stairs at its dead-end. This double staircase is relatively rare in Portland. Wouldn't it be a grand setting for a marriage? Cordon off the entire block of Lovejoy Place for the guests, who watch the happy couple emerge from the top, travel down the stairs, and speak their vows on the landing. I hope to be invited.

The stairs top off on Westover Road, next to a set of five townhomes built where a Chesapeake Bay retriever, Jake, used to play. These "Jake's Run" townhomes are from 2001, but have a 1920s, Arts-and-Crafts/Modern style. Two buildings flank an English-style courtyard. One building is three units; it's designed to look like a single home; the other building has two units, and is designed to look like a carriage house. What I love best: the fir windows and old-fashioned mitered corners—a giveaway of high-quality construction.

At the top of the stairs, turn left on Westover; walk downhill. At Westover, 25th, and Johnson, keep far right to stay walking on Westover. Cross to its east side. Ignore a staircase on your left (at Irving). On the right is where the first St. Vincent Hospital was, from 1892 to 1979. Its architect was an amazing woman, Mother Joseph Pariseau (1823-1902). St. Vincent was one of many schools and hospitals she established. She not only acquired land, she designed the buildings, acted as general contractor (she was an accomplished carpenter), and ran the financial end of the sisters' increasingly complex holdings, which she incorporated as one of Washington state's first corporations. That business she founded lives on today as the parent corporation for Providence Health and Services. Mother Joseph was treated for cancer here, in 1899, in the very hospital she had built. She died in Vancouver, at Providence Academy, another building she designed and had built. It still stands.

Walk two blocks and descend 51 stairs to Glisan. Walk out Glisan to 23rd and turn left. Food, drink, shopping, watching of dogs and people (lots of tourists): all good here in this old streetcar-era district. In 2016, businesses at 23rd and Glisan were rocked by an explosion when a contractor misread a map and dug a trench on the wrong side

Path between Overton flights

of the street. That was the side where a natural gas line was buried. In the resulting explosion, no one was injured physically. However, some businesses were decimated, and others financially hurt by the resulting road closure.

From 23rd, until point 8 on the map, follow the map, climbing and descending five staircases. The street grid is self-explanatory: numeric one direction and alphabetic the other. All streets M to P end in stairways that climb to Cornell Road. Take your time and enjoy the many beautiful, old, and creatively restored homes and apartment buildings in this end of Nob Hill.

From the bottom of the Cornell-to-Pettygrove staircase, walk downhill on Pettygrove. On your left is a hill next to Chapman Elementary School. If you haven't picnicked on that hill on September evenings, you're missing a quintessential Portland experience. Thousands of Vaux's swifts *(voxes)* use the school's brick chimney to roost on their migratory path. It happens every night for about a month, and usually a hawk shows up to add an element of villainy. When the last swallow dives into the chimney for the night, you'll feel like applauding. It's a joyous antidote to life's more complicated moments.

If you come back to picnic with the swifts, don't pee, poop, leave garbage, or park in front of the neighbors' driveways (all of which have occurred). It's more fun to park far away and walk anyway; this area offers intriguing sights in every direction.

8 Turn left into Wallace Park and wander diagonally across it.
In the park's far corner look for the sculpture, "Silver Dawn," by Manuel Izquierdo (1925-2009). After fleeing Spain at age 11 during the Spanish Civil War, he eventually landed in the US as a teenager. He learned to weld in WWII at Portland's wartime shipyards, and his smooth sculptures—this one stainless steel—are voluptuous,

touchable and *biomorphic*—free-form shapes suggestive of a living organism.

Leave Wallace Park at 25th and Raleigh, then head to Thurman for food and drink—see the map for nearby food/drink corridors.

⑨ From 24th and Thurman, walk a few steps north on 24th, past a tan-brick building that used to be the Ideal Theatre. Turn left onto an inconspicuous asphalt walkway, the second of this route's hidden paths. The path ends at a gorgeous 1912 red brick apartment building with white balconies at 1830 NW 24th Place. It's one of the best-looking old apartments in town, and hidden from sight.

Walk out 24th Place to Vaughn and follow the map or quick guide to return to the start. At Upshur and 26th are the storied Fairmount Apartments. They were built as the Fairmount Hotel, and housed visitors to Portland's 1905 World's Fair, a six-month-long extravaganza held in and around Guild's Lake. Fair attractions included Professor Barnes' educated horse; diving elk, forced to dive into a tank from 40 feet up; a Filipino village, with immigrants made to spend the day in Stone Age conditions for visitors to gawk at; and infant incubators with live babies on display. If you were standing here in 1905, you'd have been at the entrance to the fair and had better get out of the way: 11,600 people attended, on average, each day.

In the decades after the fair ended, the Fairmount fell into deep disrepair and became a flophouse. One renovation in 1998 upgraded it but left it as very affordable housing. A sale for $5.2 million and an extensive renovation in 2017-2018 has resulted in yet another loss of affordable housing for Portland's lowest income citizens.

At 27th and Upshur is the edge of a small commercial area. When Guild's Lake was turned into temporary wartime housing, this area was where families grocery shopped and got other services. Also at this intersection, look down at the ghostly outline of streetcar tracks. In 1905, after fairgoers hopped off the streetcar at the fair's entrance, the car ran west to here, and then made the curve back into town via Thurman.

At 28th, the Old Forestry Commons condos are where the world's largest log cabin once sat. Built entirely of old growth, unpeeled timbers, the 1905 Forestry Building was part of the World's Fair. It burned to the ground in 1964.

If you're a serious stair geek, detour from the route, turning right at NW 28th Place, a cute stub of a street, and walk to its dead-end for a down-and-up trip to 36 of the city's last wooden stairs.

BELLA THE CAT CLIMBS THE STAIRS

From about NW 29th, looking down to Guilds Lake and early homes in Willamette Heights. Around 1904. St. Helens Road is upslope of the lake.

STAIRS, IN ORDER ENCOUNTERED	UP OR DOWN	NUMBER
1. Vaughn at 30th to upper Vaughn	Up	32
2. Thurman to Aspen	Up	101
3. Thurman Street Bridge stairs to Forest Park entrance – 71 optional	Both	142*
4. 29th and Quimby to Cornell	Up	25
5. Cornell to Summit	Up	73
6. Summit to Westover	Up	157
7. Fairfax to Cumberland	Up	131
8. Luray Terrace to Luray Circus	Up	52
9. Summit to Lovejoy	Down	33
10. 25th Place to Westover	Up	41
11. Westover to Glisan	Down	51
12. Irving to Westover	Up	48
13. Marshall to Cornell	Up	55
14. Cornell to Northrup	Down	63
15. Overton to Cornell	Up	56
16. Cornell to Pettygrove	Down	65
17. 28th Place to Wardway – 36 optional	Both	72*
Total on route		983
*Nearby optional stairs, both up and down		1,197

RESERVOIR 5 ON MT. TABOR

Mt. Tabor

With elegant old neighborhoods rising to forested mountain slopes, Southeast Portland's Mt. Tabor has all the elements essential to a great Portland walk: big views, tall firs, beautiful homes, and plenty of stairs to drive it home: you're not in Illinois, or Texas, or Nebraska anymore.

In this 4.5-mile stair walk with 11 staircases, Portland's topographical gifts are on voluptuous display. The route gains and loses 650 feet over the course of the loop. Neighborhoods surrounding Mt. Tabor Park are residential, except for one streetcar-era commercial district, near stop 3. Other restaurant and coffee options are at the beginning and end of the route, along Stark.

IN 2018 NEW RAILINGS CAME TO MT. TABOR'S LONGEST STAIRCASE

IN 2018 NEW RAILINGS AND BIKE RAMPS IMPROVED THE
OLD 96 STEPS BETWEEN RESERVOIRS 5 AND 6

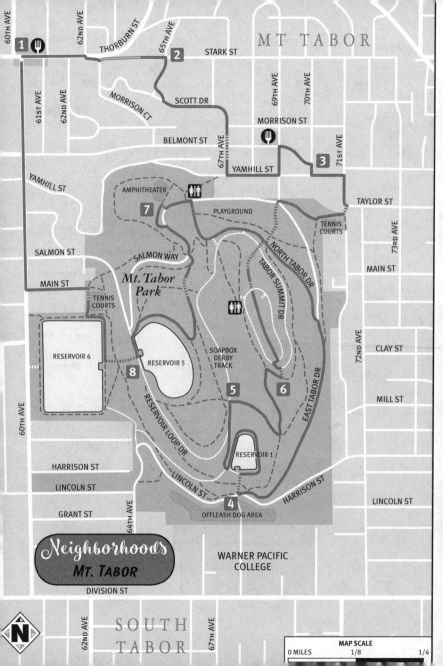

DIRECTIONS: THE QUICK GUIDE

1 ▪ ▪ Begin at SE 60th Avenue and Stark Street. Walk east on Stark alongside the historic buildings.

▪ ▪ At 61st, cross Stark—looking carefully; keep uphill on Stark.

▪ ▪ At the point where Stark (changing names to Thorburn) veers left, turn right, onto Scott Drive.

▪ ▪ Immediately go straight onto a pedestrian path left of 6205 Scott Drive.

2 ▪ ▪ The path ends at Stark west of 65th. Turn right on 65th. At a landscaped island, turn left onto Scott Drive.

▪ ▪ Just past Morrison, continue straight onto the now-gravel road, 67th. At its dead-end, descend 18 stairs to Belmont. Carefully cross Belmont and climb 21 stairs. At the top, walk straight. At Yamhill turn left.

▪ ▪ Turn left on 69th. In one block come to a small commercial area on Belmont, then keep east on a "roadway not improved" block of Belmont.

3 ▪ ▪ Turn right on 70th, make a quick left on Yamhill, then right on 71st.

▪ ▪ Where 71st ends, climb 25 stairs to a corner of Mt. Tabor Park. Veer right on a dirt path, heading to tennis courts, then follow the sidewalk to a park entrance at 69th.

▪ ▪ Climb 155 stairs to the first road that crosses this long (282-step) staircase. Turn left on it, North Tabor Drive. When East Tabor Drive comes in from the left, keep straight.

4 ▪ ▪ Pass a gate, and climb 81 stairs next to a utility building.

▪ ▪ Turn right to walk around Reservoir 1.

■■ Leave the reservoir loop at a concrete gatehouse and walk uphill on the paved road.

5 ■■ Take the first right, onto a wide gravel path. Climb. At an intersection, take the leftmost trail (the better groomed one).

6 ■■ Near the top of the mountain, the trail ends in a T. Go right, then quick left to climb 13 stairs ending at the summit loop road.

■■ Walk to the Harvey Scott sculpture, then north on lawn. Near a blue drinking fountain, descend stairs—part of the park's 282-step staircase. Keep right where the path forks and descend more flights of stairs, for a total of 127. Cross one road (Tabor Summit Drive) and immediately turn left on the next (North Tabor Drive).

■■ Stop in the visitor center, near the restrooms.

7 ■■ Descend 17 stairs into the stone amphitheater, then walk out of it alongside the basketball court, heading to a paved road.

■■ Turn right on the road; just past a painted crosswalk, turn left onto a trail where ahead you can see 30 railroad-tie stairs. Climb them and walk toward Reservoir 5 on the soapbox derby track.

■■ Take the steep trail, with steps, downhill to the right and walk around the north end of Reservoir 5 on the trail, heading to its west (downhill) side.

8 ■■ Across from Reservoir 5's gate house, descend 134 stairs to Reservoir 6.

■■ Walk alongside the reservoir to its north side and a dirt stair path near tennis courts. The path leads to the dead-end of Main Street.

■■ Walk out Main, turn right on 60th and continue to the start.

1 **Begin at SE 60th Avenue and Stark Street.** As you walk east on
Stark, investigate the historic buildings here, and perhaps plan an
after-walk meal in one of them. First is Caldera Public House at 6031.
It inhabits Thomas Graham's 1910 pharmacy. A porch restoration
revealed Mr. Graham's concrete signage for his business. The former
address, 1593, is also carved into the cement. Portland unscrambled its
jumble of street names and numbers in the early 1930s and so once in a
while you'll see buildings with two different addresses still attached to
them, usually in a transom window.

Stark Street Station, at 6045, is now a coffee house. The building
betrays its fire-station origins in the grooved cement inside and out.
Inside, horses were stabled; fire fighters bunked upstairs. When the
fire bell rang, the horses were harnessed to the wagon and the grooved
cement helped them avoid slipping as they bolted through the doorways
(now windows). On the east side, note the tower—that's where cotton
firehoses were hung to dry.

Walk east on Stark. Stop at 61st. In the northeast corner is a stone
milepost, P-4, placed probably in the 1870s. It denotes the distance
to Portland's first courthouse (Pioneer Courthouse at SW 6th and
Morrison), which was completed in 1875. Construction of Stark Street
(then called Baseline Road) began in the early 1850s, not long after the
1851 establishment of the Willamette Baseline (an east-west axis). The
baseline's counterpart is the Willamette Meridian, a north-south axis.
The intersection of these two invisible lines is the "point of origin" from
which land in Oregon and Washington is surveyed.

Baseline was later renamed for Benjamin Stark, who had purchased
part of the original Portland townsite in 1850. These stone mileposts
continue on Stark to the Sandy River, where the road has a spectacular
junction with the Historic Columbia River Highway. Learn more about
the mileposts at starkstreetmarkers.blogspot.com.

Beyond the milepost is the Midcentury Modern spire of Tabor Heights United Methodist Church, built in 1967.

Cross Stark—looking carefully. Oregon law states that every intersection, even if not marked with a crosswalk or light, is a pedestrian intersection. Not all drivers seem aware of this. Look them in the eyes, and make sure they acknowledge your existence before you cross.

Keep east (uphill) on Stark. Where Stark (becoming Thorburn) veers left, turn right onto Scott Drive and then immediately go straight on the pedestrian path left of the driveway at 6205 Scott. This three-block-long path along a telephone pole alignment is wonderfully hidden. It traverses a steep stretch of Stark where road builders gave up on being linear.

2 The path ends at Stark west of 65th. Turn right on 65th. The dark fir island of Mt. Tabor Park is ahead in the distance. In one block, at a landscaped island, turn left onto Scott Drive. The street is named for Harvey Scott, the longtime editor of the *Oregonian* newspaper. He owned the land here when it was agricultural. His statue is seen later on the walk.

At 6607 is Rancho Lando, a 1961 Midcentury Modern reinvented with a green roof and energy saving features. Its much older-than-1961 rock wall tells the tale of a side yard sold off by owners of the adjoining house.

Next to it, at 6651 is the Wells-Guthrie house, a beautiful example of Arts and Crafts architecture. It was designed in 1912, another elegant creation of Ellis Lawrence, this one for the writer Morris B. Wells, who had purchased the lot from Harvey Scott. On the right side of the street, down in the hollow, is a 1.2-acre property with a Midcentury Modern home by architect William F. Wayman. He also designed the Rice Northwest Museum of Rocks and Minerals, built in 1952 as the home of Richard and Helen Rice. If you've ever driven to the coast on

AN UPDATED 1961 RANCH

the Sunset Highway, you've seen it: a low stone ranch at the edge of a fir grove. Its no drama exterior belies the treasures inside.

Just past Morrison, continue straight onto the now-gravel road, 67th. It seems like you're trespassing, but no. Just before road's end, notice on the left a charming cottage from 1892, a time when this area was transitioning from orchards to urban neighborhood. The stairs, originally wood, led to a streetcar stop on Belmont.

Descend 18 stairs to Belmont. Belmont runs east-west in the saddle between Mt. Tabor's two peaks: one peak is Mt. Tabor Park itself and the other is the lower peak now occupied by the neighborhood you are leaving. Mt. Tabor is one of 80 Boring Lava domes and vents, volcanic eruptions that occurred west of the Cascade Mountains in Oregon and Washington (named because their densest concentration is around Boring, Oregon).

Carefully cross Belmont and climb 21 stairs. At the top walk straight. At Yamhill turn left. Here are beautiful homes from the 1900s and 1910s that back up to Mt. Tabor Park. The park was formed in

1909 with the City's purchase of 40 properties on and around the peak. Six years prior, the famous Olmsted Brothers landscape architecture firm (of Central Park fame) recommended both of Mt. Tabor's peaks be preserved as parkland.

From Yamhill turn left on 69th and in one block come to a small commercial area on Belmont. The much-lauded restaurant, Coquine occupies a 1911 commercial building that once sat adjacent to the streetcar track. Have a meal or a snack here—it's the closest café to the summit of Mt. Tabor.

From 69th and Belmont walk east on a "roadway not improved" block of Belmont. Tom Sawyer came to mind, especially when I saw the white picket fence (yeah, it's plastic, but still) and homes dating back as far as 1894 (at 6838). The tiny duplex on the left is from the 1920s, a common sight in Portland near streetcar stops. Here the streetcar wound south and then east on Yamhill.

❸ At 70th, curvy untamed Belmont ends; turn right on 70th then quick left on Yamhill. Don't miss the enormous Japanese maple *(Acer palmatum)* at 7000; always a beautiful sight in a yard, this specimen, native to Asia, is superb, perhaps dating to the home's construction in 1954. The tree's species name *palmatum* refers to the handlike shape of its leaves. Next door is a certified Backyard Habitat at 7020. Portland Audubon and its partners certify that such urban yards contain the plants that native insect and animal species evolved with and depend on.

From Yamhill turn right on 71st. Here, barricaded behind greenery is a 1909 cast stone home. Cast stone is really cast concrete, poured in forms to simulate stone block. It had its heyday in Portland in the 1910s.

Where 71st ends, climb 25 stairs to a corner of Mt. Tabor Park. At the top, veer right on a dirt path, heading to tennis courts (dating from the 1920s) and the first of many water fountains. Follow the

concrete sidewalk to a park entrance at 69th. Here join the flow of people working out on Mt. Tabor's epic 282-step staircase.

Climb 155 stairs (10 flights, but you don't need to count) to the first road. Turn left on it, North Tabor Drive. (You'll descend the top portion of the staircase later.) Walk the road along Mt. Tabor's east flank. Soon, East Tabor Drive comes in from the left. Keep straight. Mt. Tabor is the peak-of-many-roads. Henry Ford began selling his paradigm-shifting Model T auto in 1908, a year before the park's creation. The Model T was the first car middle class Americans could afford. Built during that first flush of widespread enthusiasm for auto touring, the park's roads offer drivers many curves and vistas. Every Wednesdays, cars aren't allowed in the park at all. But even then, watch out for skateboarders and bikers.

At a clearing, enjoy the over-the-rooftops views of the Montavilla neighborhood. For newcomers to Portland: pronounce those *ll*s: the name is a portmanteau formed from "Mount Tabor Villa." All those green mountains to the east and southeast are Boring lava domes. I-205 crawls along the base of one, Kelly Butte. From 1906 to the 1950s it was the site of a prison rock quarry.

4 The road starts stealing back the elevation you gained on the stairs; now you're heading around to Mt. Tabor's south side. Pass the gate, and climb 81 stairs next to a utility building. They lead to Reservoir 1, the most venerable (from 1894) of Portland's historic open-air reservoirs. The promenade around it was designed for strolling. From 1895 to 2015, the reservoir held ready-to-drink water that had fallen as rain or fog drip in the 102-square-mile Bull Run Watershed east of Portland. The water filters through old growth forests (about half of the watershed is covered in trees 350-500 year old) before it is collected in Bull Run Lake (a natural lake enlarged by a small dam), and two reservoirs downstream.

The one million Bull Run customers use 34 billion gallons of water each year, but that only represents 20 percent of the precipitation that falls in the watershed. The rest flows into the Bull Run River, then onto the Sandy River on its way to the Pacific.

The water, by the time it reached this and other open-air reservoirs, had already been treated with a bit of chlorine to disinfect it, and sodium hydroxide to raise its pH and reduce corrosion of lead and copper in household plumbing. From the open reservoirs, it flowed directly to Portlanders' taps, despite the additions of bird droppings and the Environmental Protection Agency's repeated urging of the City to cover its reservoirs.

Portland built its six open-air reservoirs between 1894 and 1911: four on Mt. Tabor (reservoirs 1, 2, 5, and 6) and two (Reservoirs 3 and 4) in Washington Park, in the West Hills. Reservoir 2 was decommissioned in 1976 and the land sold in 1990. It was at SE Division and 60th (see the map). The site is now a retirement community. The old reservoir gatehouse is now a home.

Since 2015, Portland's open-air reservoirs have been disconnected from the city's water supply, serving only decorative purposes (and birds that stop on annual migrations). The City gave up trying to convince the EPA that our reservoirs are special.

Today underground storage tanks, more secure, and less leaky, have replaced all the open-air reservoirs. Once at risk of being inelegantly capped, Mt. Tabor's reservoirs are now protected by their status on the National Register of Historic Places, living on in form, if not function.

At the top of the stairs turn right, to walk around the reservoir so you can see the spring and its altar. The artesian spring emerging from the hillside at the reservoir's north end evidently delighted the reservoir builders. They built a fountain for it, and provided an iron cup for strollers to dip and drink from. The iron ring that held the cup

One of the stone markers on Southeast Stark Street. P4 = 4 miles to the Pioneer Courthouse in downtown Portland

remains, as does an iron support for a long-gone bridge to the fountain across the gutter. Now an altar receives your offerings. The walkway around the reservoir was repaired in 2017-2018.

Near the end of the reservoir loop, leave it at the concrete gatehouse and walk uphill on the road along the reservoir's west side. Here are great vantage points to see the whole of Reservoir 1.

5 Take the first right onto a wide gravel path (opposite a nice view of Reservoir 5). Climb. At an intersection in the woods, interestingly, is a lamppost. It dates from the 1920s. Take the leftmost trail (the better groomed one). As you climb, notice the understory bushes; in fall you'll see the white berries of snowberry (*Symphoricarpos albus*), a common native shrub in the honeysuckle family. The berries are winter food for birds (but never edible for humans).

6 Near the top of the mountain, the gravel trail ends in a T. Ignore the sign telling you to turn left. Go right then take a quick left to climb 13 stairs. They lead to the loop road around the summit. It's been closed to car traffic since the 1970s. Take a moment to visit Harvey Scott (1838-1910). Perhaps Portland's most famous editorialist, Scott was an irascible badass. In his youth he cleared ground for family farms, fought Indians, logged timber, and mined for gold, growing increasingly conservative along the way. After working his way through Pacific University (he was its first graduate), he reigned for 40 years as editor of the *Oregonian*. The position gave him an effective pulpit from which to expound on his personal views

Harvey feuded openly with his ground-breaking sister, Abigail Scott Duniway (1834-1915), who founded progressive newspapers, authored many books, and battled Harvey and the culture for women's right to vote. In 1912, she cast her first ballot after Oregon gave women the right to vote. It would be eight more years before the US Constitution was amended to grant women that right.

This 1933 sculpture was created from funds provided by Harvey's widow in her will. The sculptor was Gutzon Borglum, who sculpted the faces of four presidents on Mt. Rushmore.

From Harvey, walk north on lawn sprouting tall Douglas firs to the summit. See if you can find the summit marker. The peak was purchased in 1861 by Chauncey Hosford, who farmed the peak and land around it. Around 1890 the City chose Mt. Tabor's slopes as the site for reservoirs for the new Bull Run water system.

In 1903, Portland hired the Olmsted Brothers landscape architecture firm to survey the city and recommend a system of parks and parkways that it could use as a blueprint for future development. Here is what the report said, in part, about Mt. Tabor:

> *There seems to be every reason why a portion, at least, of Mount Tabor should be taken as a public park...It is already a good deal resorted to by people for their Sunday and holiday outings...*

They recommended that the home and stable at the summit be removed, and a shelter built here, closing with this bit of paternal advice:

> *Arrangements should be made for the sale of the purest possible milk at this shelter, as nothing is better for many of the hot weather troubles of infancy than absolutely pure milk and plenty of fresh air.*

A caretaker lived on the summit in the early years of the park, until a caretaker home was built in 1920 at the Salmon Street entrance. That house is now rented out, but still owned by the City. The storybook-style restroom at the summit was restored to use in 2017, ending the decadeslong run of the portable toilet up here.

After enjoying the summit and its views to the west, find the top of the 282-step staircase (at the summit's north end, near a blue drinking fountain). After one flight down, you're on a dirt path from which round river cobbles peek out. This is the Troutdale Formation, thick (as in up to 1,600 feet deep) deposits of gravels and sand deposited by the ancient Columbia River and Cascade streams millions of years ago. Here, when Mt. Tabor was formed 200,000 years ago, magma intruded into a subsurface chamber, uplifting the Troutdale Formation, but not flowing over and burying it. Hence, river-tumbled rocks lie at the 500-foot level on the peak.

Mt. Tabor is commonly called one of the nation's few extinct volcanoes within a city's limits. In 2009, the scholarly magazine *Oregon Geology* described it less romantically: "Mt. Tabor is a Troutdale Formation structural high, with a small Boring cinder cone at its north end."

Keep right where the path forks, heading to subsequent flights of stairs, passing on your left the cap of Mt. Tabor's only buried reservoir—Reservoir 7, built in 1912. On the stairs, cross one road (Tabor Summit Drive) and immediately turn left on the next road (North Tabor Drive). On it, pass the playground, restroom and visitor center, and restrooms. The center is staffed by Friends of Mt. Tabor Park.

7 **Descend the stairs into the park's amphitheater,** the quarried-out vent of the Boring Lava dome, where rock and gas erupted at the surface. In the early 1900s, after rock had been excavated for road-building, local geologists persuaded the City to preserve the site. Take a walk around its perimeter and see the black scoria wall, the stage shaded by leaning cedars, and the beautiful, moss-covered rubble wall.

Walk out of the amphitheater along the basketball court to an opening in the rubble wall. Head up to the paved road and turn right, walking downhill under columnar firs. At a painted crosswalk, turn left onto a trail where ahead you can see a railroad-tie staircase. Climb its 30 stairs and either follow main park trails (see the map, south of Salmon Way) or walk toward Reservoir 5 briefly on the straightaway road then turn downhill on a steep, less groomed trail.

This wide road at the top of Reservoir 5 is a soapbox derby track built in 1956. Races were held until 1965. For kids. In 1997, the first PDX Adult Soapbox Derby was held in the park. It happens every year in August—not on that flat straightaway, but running from near the top of the mountain down to the base of Reservoir 5.

Head to the west side of Reservoir 5, to its gatehouse. Reservoir 5 was built in 1911. In winter look for bufflehead ducks enjoying their city park.

8 **Here take a set of super-steep stairs, with handrails installed in 2018.** Notice the very tall giant sequoia to the left, above Reservoir 6. It was planted in 1913 by the park's designer (and Portland's park superintendent) Emanuel Mische.

At the bottom of the stairs, at Reservoir 6, walk its east and north sides to a dirt path near the tennis courts. The path leads to 12 railroad-tie stairs, topping off at a beautiful dead-end: Main Street. Here leave the park. Walk out Main to 60th. If you want to hit the last major park stair, at 60th, turn left and visit the 43-step staircase between 60th and Reservoir 6 (see the map). At 6133 SE Main is a grand Craftsman; at 6115 a huge and beautiful tulip poplar (*Liriodendron tulipifera*)—a native east of the Mississippi that can grow to 150 feet tall. In spring look up to see its green and yellow tuliplike flowers perched above the leaves.

At 60th, turn right and enjoy old homes and trees in the half-mile walk back to the start.

1 Flight in Mt. Tabor's longest staircase, with its old railings

STAIRS, IN ORDER ENCOUNTERED	UP OR DOWN	NUMBER
1. 67th near Scott Drive to Belmont	Down	18
2. Belmont to 67th near Yamhill	Up	21
3. 71st into Mt. Tabor Park	Up	25
4. Yamhill to North Tabor Drive	Up	155
5. East Tabor Drive to Reservoir 1	Up	81
6. top-of-trail stairs to summit near Harvey Scott	Up	13
7. Summit of park to North Tabor Drive	Down	127
8. Visitor Center area to amphitheater	Down	17
9. Trail to near Reservoir 5	Up	30
10. Reservoir 5 to Reservoir 6	Down	134
11. Reservoir 6 to Main Street	Up	12
12. Reservoir 6 to 60th – 43 optional	Both	86*
Total on route		**633**
Nearby optional stairs, both up and down		719

VISIBLE FROM ALL OVER PORTLAND, THE GARGANTUAN
STONEHENGE TOWER SITS ATOP ONE OF PORTLAND'S HIGHEST PEAKS

Hillsdale to Council Crest Park

T his 4.6-mile stair walk explores the sunny, south-facing slopes of the West Hills. Climb from a cool midcentury business district via seven staircases, five hidden paths and one isolated pedestrian bridge to Portland's highest point, Council Crest Park. The sculptural, 625-foot Stonehenge tower atop a second, 1,000-foot peak is a recurring presence as you climb. Elevation gain is 550 feet.

The return route is equally fascinating: a posh neighborhood, a tower farm, and an old wagon road dropping through woods back to the start. Afterwards, have a meal at a brewpub, cafe, or the Hillsdale Food Park, and visit the elegant library. In summer, pack a swimsuit and towel, and stretch out at Wilson Pool. It's operated by Portland Parks & Recreation on a hilltop where cows once grazed.

Seven TriMet bus lines (44, 45, 54, 55, 56, 61, 64) stop at the starting point. Ride the bus, explore, eat, drink, swim and have a mini-vacation in your hometown.

Pick a clear day if you want the best views from Council Crest Park. Choose a Sunday, to eat and drink at the Hillsdale Farmers' Market. It's in the Mary Rieke School lot, south of the start, and is open every Sunday, or alternate Sundays, depending on the month.

ON SOUTHWEST 18TH DRIVE, NATURE GETS THE LAST WORD

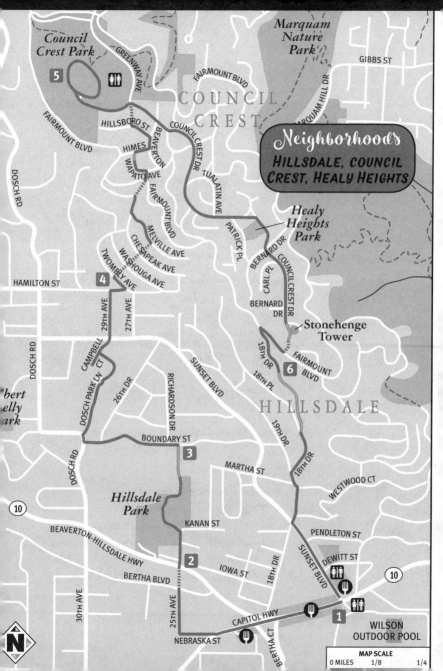

DIRECTIONS: THE QUICK GUIDE

1 ▪ ▪ ▪   Start at Sunset Blvd and Capitol Hwy and walk west on the highway's sidewalk.

▪ ▪ ▪   At Bertha Court, cross to the southwest corner (under the Hillsdale sign). Pass over Bertha Blvd and by restaurants in vintage buildings. Cross Capitol Hwy at a marked crosswalk and turn left, walking west in the bike lane a short way.

▪ ▪ ▪   Turn right on Nebraska, then right on 25th. Where it ends at Bertha Blvd, take a stair path of 97 stairs down into and up out of a creek valley, to Beaverton Hillsdale Hwy.

2 ▪ ▪ ▪   Cross the highway at a signalized crosswalk. Stay north on 25th, and come to Hillsdale Park and Robert Gray Middle School. Walk north on bark chip paths through the field to a hidden pedestrian bridge over a canyon. Cross.

3 ▪ ▪ ▪   At bridge's end, turn left on Boundary; in 0.3 mile, turn right on Dosch Road and immediately right on Dosch Park Lane. Where it ends at Campbell Court, walk left to its dead-end.

▪ ▪ ▪   Walk out Campbell Court to Sunset Blvd; cross it and walk north on 29th one block, then right on Hamilton and quick left on Twombly.

4 ▪ ▪ ▪   Just past 4424, begin ascending a stair path of 64 stairs; along the path cross Washouga and Chesapeak. At the third street, Melville, turn left off the path. Walk past a half dozen homes then right on Chesapeak. Walk 250 feet to a wooden staircase. Climb 69 stairs. At the top, cross Fairmount and keep uphill on Wapato. Where it Ts, turn left and walk to its dead-end and beyond, to Himes, and turn right. Turn left on Beaverton and left on Hillsboro. Past 2747, climb 50 stairs to Council Crest Drive, turn left and follow the road to Council Crest Park.

5 From the park, follow Council Crest Drive downhill 1.1 mile. Pass Healy Heights Park. After Carl Place, pass water tanks and keep straight on a path next to the red and white Stonehenge radio tower.

6 The path ends at 17 stairs down to Fairmount. Turn right, then left on 18th Drive. Keep downhill on it as it becomes a pedestrian path and then residential again.

After 18th Place and 19th Drive come in on the right, cross Martha and keep downhill. Turn left on Sunset Blvd. In 0.3 mile, you've returned to the start.

1 **Start at Sunset Blvd and Capitol Hwy, in Hillsdale Town Center.**
At this spot in 1851 John Slavin farmed, and operated a forge and rock quarry. His home was a few steps uphill, near where Oregon's first brewpub now sits. The Hillsdale Brewery and Public House opened in 1984. In 1985, when the law passed allowing beer to be made and sold in the same location (for the first time since Prohibition), it became the McMenamin brothers' first brewpub. Now they have 59 pubs, 12 hotels, and 9 theaters. The library, uphill from the pub, is where Slavin built his windmill.

Capitol Highway was built in the 1880s as a wagon road between Portland and Oregon's capitol, Salem. This was dairy country then. Both Wilson High and Mary Rieke Elementary—just south of this intersection—are on pastureland once grazed by cattle. The last dairy in Hillsdale milked its last cow in the 1980s. At this intersection, the Portland Ballet occupies a former maintenance building for dairy trucks.

Walk west on the sidewalk along Capitol Hwy. Though most of the shopping/dining center dates from the 1950s, the Mexican restaurant at 6319 began life in 1928 as a feed-and-seed store serving dairy farmers.

At Capitol Hwy and Bertha Court, cross to the southwest corner (under the Hillsdale sign). This is the Bertha Triangle. Here was Bertha Station, a stop on the Red Electric train line that ran from Portland to Corvallis from 1915 to 1929.

Pass over Bertha Blvd (the former train alignment), pass by restaurants in vintage buildings, and cross Capitol Hwy at a marked crosswalk. Continue west in the bike line a short way, then turn right on Nebraska, and right on 25th. In a few blocks 25th ends at Bertha Blvd. Here, take one of Portland's newest staircases: 57 stairs down to Fanno Creek, and 40 stairs up. This stair path is the result of years of advocacy by SW Trails to create a safe route to school for neighborhood kids. In 2018, with just $23,000 in City of Portland funds plus hours of volunteer labor, SW Trails improved this once steep,

VOLUNTEERS WORKING WITH SW TRAILS WERE JUST ABOUT DONE
BUILDING THE 25TH AVE STEPS IN JANUARY 2018

balancing-act of a trail with rail-tie stairs. Each stair took volunteers about one hour to build.

This route covers several crossings of Fanno Creek's tributary streams. After you do this hill walk, you may want to bike the Fanno Creek Trail and follow the creek as it meanders through the flat Tualatin Valley to its confluence with the Tualatin River, in Tigard. It's a beautiful, easy ride.

2 **At the stair path's end, cross Beaverton Hillsdale Hwy at the signalized crosswalk. Stay north on 25th and come to Hillsdale Park and Robert Gray Middle School.** At Kanan are two options: the first option has you turning right, then left on 23rd. Near the north end of the school, descend 69 stairs to a path running along the edge of the forest. Here, find the pedestrian bridge. (Also on 23rd are the optional 20 stairs up to Sunset Drive).

The other option: hang left at 25th and Kanan and follow trails northward around the fenced playing field. This puts you alongside a popular dog off-leash area, so you might get some wet noses investigating you. Follow the bark chip trail around the fenced area (keeping right at a fork), and into the woods north of it, where you'll see the bridge.

Make your way to the pedestrian bridge. Below runs Trillium Creek in a canyon of western redcedar, bigleaf maple, and Douglas fir. The 204-foot-long bridge was built in 1953. A rappelling teenager in the 1980s triggered installation of the mouse-run cage that envelops the bridge. Perhaps some day the barrier could be re-envisioned with a bit more finesse. That'd be a nice culmination to the restoration work in this forest, done by neighbors. Working with a conservation plan crafted by the West Multnomah Soil and Water Conservation District, they've removed invasives and planted native plants, restoring the habitat for fish, wildlife, and humans.

3 **At bridge's end, walk out to Boundary and turn left.** In 0.3 mile, turn right on Dosch Road and immediately right on Dosch

Park Lane, a private road. Please respect the generosity of residents in allowing passage. This is part of the 17-acre Henry E. Dosch estate once called Villa Eichenhof. A few dozen homes here were developed after parts of the estate were sold in the 1980s. After a roundabout, come to a cluster of Portland Heritage Trees, at or near the original Dosch home, at 4825, which dates from the 1880s. Henry E. Dosch (1841-1925) built it soon after he and wife Marie bought the land, part of which was an existing apple orchard. Look for a 150-foot incense cedar, 100- and 125-feet tall Ponderosa pines, a Sitka Spruce (visible from Campbell Court), and other big trees planted by Dosch.

He was an Oregon horticultural pioneer, promoting walnut production in the Willamette Valley. A member of the state's first Board of Horticulture for decades, he wrote *Horticulture in Oregon* in 1904. He purchased this land in the 1880s because it had a large orchard on it. Dosch descendants still live in the family home.

Where Dosch Park Lane ends at Campbell Court, turn left to walk to its dead-end. The tree in the turnaround is the oldest apple tree in Oregon. Albert Kelly planted it, a Yellow Bellflower, in 1850 in his orchard here. The tree came from the Luelling and Meek Fruit Tree Nursery in Milwaukie. Henderson Luelling brought 700 grafted fruit trees west in 1847 to establish a nursery. That nursery was at what is today the Waverly Country Club. This tree, along with other historic orchard trees, is maintained, gratis, by a local tree service.

Walk out Campbell Court to Sunset. Cross it and walk north on unsigned 29th for one block, then turn right on Hamilton and quick left on Twombly.

4 Almost immediately, just past 4424, turn right into a driveway and begin ascending a stair path of 64 stairs that runs uphill on a public right-of-way. On the stair path, cross Washouga and Chesapeak. At the topmost street, Melville, turn left. Walk past a half dozen homes, then turn right on Chesapeak and walk 250 feet to a steep, maybe-muddy path to 69 wooden stairs, across from

4108. Climb. At the top, carefully cross Fairmount and continue uphill on Wapato. Where it Ts, turn left and walk to its dead-end, where the sidewalk continues to Himes. Turn right, then make a quick left on Beaverton and left on Hillsboro. Just past 2747, climb 50 stairs to Council Crest Drive at Greenway. Turn left and follow Council Crest Drive uphill to Council Crest Park.

Views are panoramic here at Portland's highest peak: four Cascade volcanoes, the Columbia River, and much of the city. In the other direction are beautiful views of the Tualatin Valley and Coast Range. The water tank is where an observatory once stood when this was an amusement park (1909-1929). Patrons arrived via the streetcar that stopped at Greenway and Council Crest Drive.

⑤ From the park, follow Council Crest Drive 1.1 mile. Homes are wonderfully varied in age, size, and style. Pass Healy Heights Park. Soon after Carl Place, enter a tower farm of radio antennas. At the gate near Portland Water Bureau's Bertha water tanks, pass through the pedestrian portal. The house at 4636 was built in 1947 as a transmitter building for an FM station; its radio tower once stood on the building's north side (where the deck is). The current owner converted the building to a home; its address numbers used to be the "On-Air" sign.

This area, almost as high as Council Crest, was initially home to radio station studios; now only their antennas remain. The largest is the beautiful, sculptural Stonehenge Tower, a 625-foot behemoth. Built in 1990 to consolidate many smaller towers, it's unguyed—no wires holding it in place like the large towers at Sylvan Hill. Instead, it's self-supporting, with concrete rising inside the three legs to the 400-foot level. The height allows radio waves to project outward, above nearby human activity. It is taller than Portland's tallest building, the Wells Fargo Center.

Caution: the tower reaches to 1,625 feet in elevation. Ice and snow in Portland are extremely elevation-dependent. Even if there's no ice where you're standing below the tower, there could be ice above, if conditions are right. When it falls off the tower, it could be deadly. So use care in winter when exploring around the tower. But if it's safe, do go see the view from the parklike area east of the tower's base—walk behind the former radio station studio that's now a transmitter building for many local stations. Views are spectacular.

The colorful house near the tower was built in the early 1950s by a radio engineer, Harold Singleton, with salvaged materials from the Vanport Flood. KBOO's transmitter was in the garage of this house the first eight years of its existence.

Look up at the tower: inside the center column is a ladder that climbs about 500 feet, to the top platform.

When you're done looking around, head back to the water tanks and then walk south on a narrow, muddy-in-winter path along the arbor vitae hedge. At a fence line, continue downhill between houses. The path ends at 17 steep stairs. This public right-of-way was overgrown but wrestled into usability by SW Trails folks. I love them. It's not pretty (yet) but it gets the job done.

6 The stairs ends at Fairmount. Cross it carefully (watching for bikes and cars on this popular work-out loop). Turn right. In 500 feet, turn left onto private-looking 18th Drive. It's indeed public. It's a dead-end for cars, but not walkers or bikers. Keep on it as this former farm-to-market road travels downhill. Gorgeous, columnar Douglas firs here have been molested by English ivy. Hopefully, removal is in somebody's plans.

At two homes (the one on the right is 4939), it feels like you're trespassing, but you're not. Walk straight, into the driveway at 4939 and continue on an unpaved pedestrian path. This is another SW

Trails success story; the group and nearby neighbors worked to preserve access when this section of roadway was threatened by development. Neighbors purchased the property and later resold it to the Columbia Land Trust, a land conservancy. The site is called Nicolai Woods.

Keep downhill on 18th Drive as the path ends and the route again becomes residential. Keep straight (downhill) where 18th Place and 19th Drive come in on the right. Cross Martha and keep downhill on 18th Drive.

Turn left on Sunset and enjoy new sidewalks, a vast improvement over the gravel shoulder once here. In 0.3 mile, you're back at the start, where food, drink, and maybe a swim are next up.

THE PEDESTRIAN BRIDGE OVER TRILLIUM CREEK, WITH ITS ANTI-RAPELLING CAGE

STAIRS, IN ORDER ENCOUNTERED	UP OR DOWN	NUMBER
1. 25th from Bertha Blvd to creek 25th, from creek to Beaverton Hillsdale Hwy	Down Up	57 40
2. 23rd into Robert Gray/Hillsdale Park	Down	69
3. 23rd to Sunset Drive – 20 optional	Both	40*
4. Twombly to Melville	Up	64
5. Chesapeak to Fairmount	Up	69
6. Hillsboro to Council Crest Drive	Up	50
7. 19th to Fairmount	Down	17
Total on route		**366**
***Nearby optional stairs, both up and down**		**406**

A PEDESTRIAN BRIDGE SPANS A SECLUDED CANYON NEAR
AINSWORTH SCHOOL IN PORTLAND HEIGHTS

Portland Heights

P ortland Heights is one of the city's best neighborhoods for walking because, block after block, homes and landscapes are high-end and gorgeous. The neighborhood has two personalities: a right-angled, sedate half that adheres to Portland's rectangular street grid, and a curvy, voluptuous half where streets wrap around peaks and insinuate themselves into ravines. This stair walk meanders around the curvy places.

On this 3.6-mile loop (with a suggested option to extend to 5.0 miles) are four hidden paths and a pedestrian bridge, 12 staircases, and occasional distant views. It gains and loses about 600 feet in elevation.

With so many homes to stop and admire, plus a mid-walk lunch and browse at the poshest consignment store in town (at Vista and Spring), it's a perfect urban adventure. TriMet's bus 51 runs weekday mornings until about 9 a.m., and weekday afternoons starting about 2:30 p.m. It stops near the walk's starting point. There's no weekend service.

FRIENDS CLIMB STEPS IN THE AINSWORTH GREENSPACE ON THE WAY BACK TO CLASS.

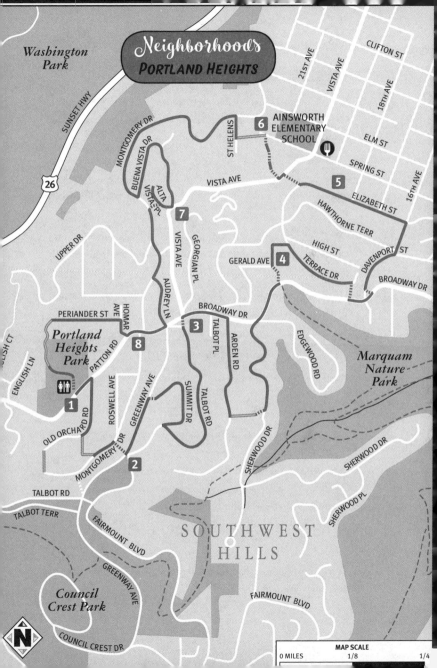

Directions: The Quick Guide

1. ▪▪▪ From Portland Heights Park (Patton and Old Orchard roads), turn left (northeast) onto Patton. Cross to Old Orchard on the painted crosswalk, and walk uphill on it.

   ▪▪▪ Past 2766, turn left on a path that leads to a driveway on Montgomery Drive. Turn left onto Montgomery and walk to 2860. Climb 86 stairs on the uphill side. At the top, Greenway, turn left.

2. ▪▪▪ Walk Greenway to 36 stairs opposite 2770. Cross the road carefully; climb to Summit Drive's dead-end, walk its length and turn left on Talbot Road.

3. ▪▪▪ Follow Talbot to 23 stairs; descend to Patton, Vista and Broadway Drive. Turn right onto Broadway Drive.

   ▪▪▪ Turn right onto Arden Road. Past 2490 take the driveway/ stair path to Sherwood Drive and turn left.

   ▪▪▪ Turn right on Broadway Drive, walking the shoulder to 2222. Cross carefully then continue downhill to 44 stairs. Climb stairs to Gerald.

4. ▪▪▪ Turn right on Gerald, then right on Terrace Drive. At its dead-end, descend 65 stairs to Broadway Drive. Carefully cross to walk downhill more safely on the one wide shoulder. Walk to 1610, look carefully and cross back; head uphill to 37 stairs to Davenport. Climb and turn right.

   ▪▪▪ Turn left on 16th, then left on Elizabeth.

5. ▪▪▪ Beyond 18th, cross to Elizabeth's north side; past 1939, descend 77 stairs to an elevated sidewalk. Turn left onto it, and cross Vista at a crosswalk.

- Descend 24 stairs to the Ainsworth School Annex. Cross the paved lot; descend 35 stairs and sidewalk through the Ainsworth Greenspace to Spring's dead-end.

6 ■ Turn left and cross an elevated walkway to St. Helens Court; turn right on it and left on Montgomery.

- Turn left on Buena Vista Drive.

7 ■ Buena Vista ends at Vista. Turn right on Vista and immediately right on Alta Vista Place.

- Descend 59 stairs to Montgomery; turn left and pass Upper Drive and an alley; turn left on Audrey Lane, then right on Patton.

8 ■ At Homar, either stay on Patton to return to the start or do the following:

- Turn right on Homar, left on Periander. At its dead-end, take the path and follow it through woods south (ignoring side paths descending into the ravine), where it leads to an opening in the chain link fence at Portland Heights Park. Climb 35 stairs to the top of the park and Patton Road.

1 Begin at Portland Heights Park, at about elevation 730 feet. The parking lot and bike rack are west of the park restroom. Turn left (northeast) onto Patton. For the crossing of Patton to Old Orchard Road, it's safest to use the painted crosswalk a short way east of the park. Walk uphill on Old Orchard. The building at the crosswalk is the rare commercial structure in Portland Heights. In 1902, Gottlieb Strohecker opened a grocery here on his land. He'd been farming here and the Sylvan area since 1880. The store operated until 2015. At the other end of the crosswalk is a giant California redwood. Not native here, it nevertheless appears to like the climate.

The land here (and land that's now Portland Heights Park), was owned by a badass-turned-captain-of-industry, Tyler Woodward. Born in 1835 in Vermont, he came west looking for gold at age 26 in Eastern Oregon. By 1864 after finding some nuggets, he purchased a stock of general merchandise and miners' supplies, loaded it onto a train of mules and set off for Western Montana, to the Stinking Water mines, where he set up business in Hell Gate (now a ghost town).

He found time to be on the local vigilante law-enforcement detail. He was, as one biographer noted, "familiar with the characters infesting the mining camps." In 1870, at age 35, with plenty of enemies and other opportunists populating the landscape, he lit off for Spokane on his horse. With $30,000 in gold stashed in his saddlebags, it must have been a nerve-wracking trip. That'd be over $500,000 today. From Spokane he left for Portland, presumably via stagecoach.

Once here, he traded some of his gold for the real estate you're standing on, among other speculative land purchases. During his ownership, cherry trees were planted here. He married Mary J. Ross (daughter of the Ross Island pioneer), and is credited with laying out Fairmount Blvd. He also headed a bank and streetcar company. The Woodwards' only daughter, Mayannah Woodward Seeley, and her husband, Boudinot,

SW Greenway Ave has one of the city's last wooden sidewalks

sold this land to a developer in the 1920s, who memorialized the orchard it had once been.

The road offers a view of the radio tower atop Council Crest, Portland's highest peak (in city limits) at 1,073 feet.

Past 2766, take a steep, uphill gravel path that lead to a driveway on Montgomery Drive. Walk out the driveway to the street and turn left. Walk a few houses to 86 stairs on the uphill side, at 2860. Climb. These wooden stairs led to a streetcar that ran along Greenway from 1904 to 1950. Until 1929, the streetcar line ended at an amusement park atop Council Crest, a few blocks from here. (See the map; it's now Council Crest Park.)

Amusement parks at the end of streetcar lines were common in the 1910s and 1920s. They created weekend demand for the lines. Oaks Amusement Park in Sellwood is another example; it's the only Portland streetcar-era amusement park still operating. Another one was in Canemah (now Old Canemah Park in Oregon City). On the Columbia, Jantzen Beach followed two other streetcar-era amusement parks: Columbia Beach and Lotus Isle (now reduced to a tiny city park).

The Council Crest line was Portland's last operating streetcar line, and these stairs are some of the city's last wooden stairs; they will be replaced with metal when the time comes.

2 At the top of the stairs turn left on Greenway, walking on the wooden sidewalk, another relic of the streetcar era. As you walk downhill, good views appear on the left of Washington Park and the radio towers off Skyline Blvd. The furthest ones are on TV Hill (elevation 1,275 feet), a Boring Lava dome that intruded itself into the Tualatin Mountains.

Boarded up sections on the concrete wall across the street were gates that provided streetcar access to residents on the street above. The homes were built in the 1900s and 1910s, soon after the streetcar went

in. Residents could walk out of their back yards to streetcar stops on Greenway, and head to their downtown offices. One opening remains unboarded, with a sweet old iron gate.

Stay on Greenway to a staircase opposite 2770 (a fire hydrant at its base). Cross carefully and climb 36 stairs to Summit Drive's dead-end. Follow lovely Summit as it curls around an 820-foot-high peak.

As the road curves northeast, a home with a torii—a Japanese temple gate—hospitably shares its fine views with walkers. Mt. Adams rises above Washington's hills. Don't miss the spectacular twin European beech trees at 2755. Because of their size they're usually seen only on large-lot properties like this one. Across from them, at 2758, sits a modern home (circa 2015) perching on the shoulders of a 1921 home, which fronts on the street below; you'll see it in a minute.

Where Summit descends to meet Talbot Road, turn left onto Talbot. Look around a sometimes-overhanging hedge for cars, and carefully cross to the other side of Talbot. So much to see here: intriguing private stairs, beautiful landscaping, and pedestrian-friendly hedges. Just past 2658, look left to see the old 1921 home heroically bearing its burden of the two-story addition. Because this house is on a through lot—i.e., the home fronts on two separate streets and the frontages don't intersect, and it's also super steep, the new home atop the old doesn't seem as incongruous as it might sound.

3 **Follow Talbot to the top of a staircase. Descend 23 stairs to Patton Road, Vista, and Broadway Drive.** Vista is the point where Patton changes name to Broadway Drive. Here is a Nellie Bubbler. Locally famous timber baron and philanthropist Simon Benson usually gets all the credit for Portland's sidewalk water fountains, even those that came much later than his original bequest to purchase fountains. But this little single bubbler is named for donor Nellie Robinson (1843-1921). She moved to Portland in her thirties in 1877. When she died at age 78, she bequeathed $2,000 to the city, specifically for water

RAY LOSEY'S TOTEM POLE ON SHERWOOD DRIVE

A BACKYARD GATE ON GREENWAY AVENUE ONCE LED TO THE STREETCAR

fountains. Robinson's original bubbler here had an attached dog bowl. In her will she stipulated the fountain should have a basin where "God's dumb creatures might slake their thirst." Vandalism of that fountain led to its removal in the late 1950s. This one, sans dog bowl, was installed in 1960. See the Portland Water Bureau site to find other Nellie Bubblers.

From the bubbler, turn right onto Broadway Drive, then right onto Arden Road. Arden and the next road on the route, Sherwood, penetrate the forested canyon that is now preserved as Marquam Nature Park. An especially charming home at 2412 makes an already wonderful walk even better.

The home at 2421, while not viewable due to the landscaping, is worth a stop to thank the women who built it, for their huge contribution to Oregon's conservation ethos. It was built in 1926 by Caroline (1873-1970) and Maria Louise Flanders (1876-1958), daughters of Captain George H. and Maria Flanders. They had grown up in a mansion their parents built in 1882 at NW 19th and Flanders. The sisters sold that property in the 1920s to Congregation Beth Israel. It's now the site of Temple Beth Israel.

The women were great philanthropists: in 1933 they donated 186 acres of oceanfront for the creation of Ecola State Park, one of the state's most scenic sections of coastline. Their action inspired others to donate or sell land, expanding the park's acreage, and igniting an era of excitement and growth for the cash-strapped state park system. Unlike most donors of that time (or today), the sisters did not want their names attached to the land that had been in their family for forty or so years. Instead, they insisted the new park retain the land's historic name. *Ecola* is believed to mean "whale" in Chinook Jargon.

I recommend walking all the way to Arden's dead-end because the homes are beautiful, and then taking up the directions again:

Past 2490 SW Arden is a hydrant and an asphalt-paved driveway-like path. Take it. It ends at eight stairs down to Sherwood Drive.

A gardener, immortalized, in Portland Heights

The route turns left on Sherwood, but if you feel like exploring, go right on Sherwood to its end (0.5 mile from here) to see how this road evolves from being populated by century old homes to newer homes as it pierces further into the canyon. Don't miss the home a few steps away, at 2520. Its 17-foot totem pole was carved from Western redcedar by sculptor Ray Losey. He carved it decades earlier but it sat in a warehouse; in 2010 he refurbished, repainted, and erected it in his yard. In a 2011 Oregonian article, Mr. Losey says of the pole, "It is a gift to the public." Take a moment to enjoy that gift.

Turn left on Sherwood and walk to Broadway Drive. It's dangerous because no sidewalks, many blind curves, and fast traffic. Turn right, walking the right shoulder to 2222, then look and listen for cars before crossing. Continue downhill (right) past a few homes, then climb 44 stairs to Gerald.

Here you see a SW Trails 6 sign. It marks one of many Southwest Portland urban trails created by citizen-led SW Trails.

4 **At the top of the stairs, turn right on Gerald, walk past 1920s homes, then turn right on Terrace Drive,** which sits on the south-facing, sunny flank of a peak, with Mt. Hood appearing over its dead-end. The roadway was elevated here at some point after homes were built in the 1900s and 1910s, resulting in long steep staircases down to some of the houses.

Walk to Terrace's dead-end and descend 65 stairs to Broadway Drive. Carefully cross it so you can walk downhill more safely on the south side's wide shoulder. Walk to 1610. This is one of Portland Heights' oldest homes, dating from 1896. When it was built, this road—then called Patton Road—was a much slower affair. No gleaming Mercedes or BMWs flew by, just horses and carriages coming over the hill from the farms in what are now Hillsdale, Raleigh Hills and Garden Home. The Patton Cemetery is where the road's namesake, early settler

Matthew Patton is buried. It offers a quiet space amid modern frenzy on Old Scholls Ferry Road.

From the house at 1610, cross Broadway Drive with care and head back uphill a short bit to 37 stairs. Climb and turn right on Davenport. At an 1894-vintage home at 1600, turn left on 16th. Halfway up the block, stop and turn. Right here you're cresting the hill. Behind is Marquam Gulch and Council Crest with its tower; ahead is downtown Portland.

From 16th, turn left on Elizabeth. Homes on the left sit increasingly higher above, flanking a small peak at elevation 770 feet. That peak was once called Markle Hill for the developer who built a mansion atop it (see that mansion on Hawthorne Terrace if you want to investigate). As you walk west on Elizabeth, you're descending to the beginning of a small drainage, a creek that begins as springs flowing off the peak between 17th and 18th. Just before you reach 17th, notice the fantastic jumbled wall of clinker brick erupting with sedum.

From 17th, look up to see evidence of landslides in the steep headscarp (cliff) from which the land gave way and slid downhill. The homes at 1704 and 1710 have a very stout concrete wall and jaw-dropping staircases to be surmounted before one can enjoy what must be killer views. They were built in 1909.

The home at 1800 was built in 1890. Next to its garage used to be a staircase that led to a Japanese teahouse on the street far above, Hawthorne Terrace. When developers began promoting lot sales in Portland Heights, people would take the cable car from the flats of Goose Hollow up to the Heights. The cable car ended one block from here, at Spring and 18th. Passengers would walk up to the staircase, climb it, and have tea while enjoying views from Markle Hill. Many liked what they saw and bought lots to build on.

Beginning with that cable railway access in 1890, Portland Heights has always been an aspirational neighborhood. Unlike many now-expensive Portland neighborhoods, it never suffered an era when city planners and their developer pals placed it on the chopping block for urban renewal or tried to run a highway through it.

5 **Beyond 18th, cross to Elizabeth's north side.** During a cold, dry December, water flowed from holes in the curb below 1800 Elizabeth, forming a wide, thin ice slick, evidence of the springs. The springs, which may have been responsible for the landslide long ago, gave rise to the name of the street one block downhill.

Across from 1929, don't overlook a spectacular staircase descending from the home above to a concrete bench, perhaps placed there to enjoy the view of Mt. St. Helens. That view disappeared in the early 1950s when a quartet of one-story homes was built here.

Past 1939, find 77 stairs hiding in a laurel hedge. Descend to an elevated sidewalk. Turn left on it, cross Vista at a crosswalk, then descend 24 curving stairs to a freestanding classroom at Ainsworth School Annex. Turn right, walking across the lot; descend 13 stairs to a beautiful forested area, the Ainsworth Greenspace. Follow the curving sidewalk to more stairs and continue, passing a stone-seat amphitheater under tall firs. Descend more stairs to Spring's dead-end. The original (1913) and still used Ainsworth School is ahead.

If you want lunch, Vista Spring Café is one block east. The building it occupies was originally the Portland Heights Grocery, built in 1908 along the streetcar line. A 1910 Oregonian help-wanted ad for the store looks for "A first-class boy to drive delivery wagon." I can only imagine what "first-class" might have been code for excluding. In the 1920s the grocery was run by Ivar Bohnsen who built the charming cottages (rebranded today as tiny homes) just downhill. In the 1950s, the grocery was owned by the Strohecker family. The café has been a neighborhood landmark since 1986. Next door to it is a wonderful antique and consignment store full of treasures from the neighborhood.

6 At Spring's dead-end, find one of the city's rare pedestrian options: a trestle walkway across a steep ravine. Walk across to St. Helens Court. Investigate its charming dead-end (on the left) then walk out to Montgomery. Turn left. Pass a couple of homes, then notice the wall and grounds on the left; they belong to the 2-acre Frank J. and Maude Louise Cobbs estate. It's one of the city's most famous homes, almost 15,000 square feet designed in the Jacobethan style in 1917 by the famous A.E. Doyle. It took two years to build and then the Cobbs sailed off to Europe and Asia, buying $145,000 worth of items to fill it with.

The son of a Cadillac, Michigan lumberman, Cobbs inherited the start of his fortune. His company, Cobbs & Mitchell, first bought Oregon timberlands in 1904, namely, old growth timber in the Siletz River watershed near the Oregon Coast. In 1912 Cobbs moved here to supervise the logging operations in the Siletz basin. A company town, Valsetz, was incorporated in 1919, housing workers who cut the old growth trees and milled them into timbers. By the 1950s, the ancient trees had been largely extirpated; so the mill was converted to plywood and veneer. By the early 1980s, with successive generations of logging, marketable trees were no longer close enough to the mill to make transport economically feasible. In 1983, the mill closed for good. The town Valsetz was intentionally burned to the ground and planted over. (Fun fact: Valsetz was coined from *Valley* and *Siletz*.)

A tiny remnant of that old growth forest escaped harvest; it can be seen, with much arduous driving over rough roads, near the site of Valsetz. Owned by the Bureau of Land Management, the 51-acre forest remnant is called the Valley of the Giants.

Looking across Montgomery, the Cobbs enjoyed a quiet view down into a forested canyon. Now the Sunset Highway roars like the ocean in that canyon. Originally their estate ran down the hill all the way to Canyon Road, then a two-lane market road between Portland's waterfront and the agricultural Tualatin Valley. Today that humble road is buried, deep under the fill excavated from the Vista Ridge Tunnels in the 1960s.

Continue on Montgomery: just opposite the Cobbs estate driveway look right to a roadway marked by stone columns; below here the estate stables were located, with road access from Canyon Road. That roadway now ends at a gleaming white Modernist home by architect Robert L. Thompson, notable for his firm's creation of the Nike World Headquarters campus in Beaverton.

As you walk, on the left are homes high above, on Buena Vista Drive. Anytime a developer breaks out the Spanish for *"good view, high view, or mountain view"* it's a good idea to investigate.

So turn left onto Buena Vista Drive and walk its super scenic semi-circle. As you walk around, look up at the home that occupies the peak; it's another A.E. Doyle creation, this one in 1925 for rich rancher John G. (Jack) Edwards. He came here from Wales, and owned the massive Hay Creek Ranch east of Madras, Oregon in the 1890s to early 1900s.

EVEN THE GARBAGE IS ELEGANT ON SW BUENA VISTA DR.

He called this home Pen-y-Bryn, Welsh for "crest of the hill." The roof slate is from Wales.

Buena Vista is an architectural smorgasbord. Every home arrayed around the 720-foot peak is a different style: Dutch Colonial, Arts and Crafts, Georgian, Tudor, Spanish Colonial Revival.

7 **Buena Vista drops you off onto Vista. Turn right and immediately come to Alta Vista Place; turn right.**

At the end of this tiny street is the Edwards home, prefaced by three newer homes built in the 1950s and 1960s, likely from sold-off portions of the Edwards property.

On Alta Vista Place, descend 59 stairs on your left. Note the impressive gabion wall on your right that supports a parking area for a home on Alta Vista. A gabion wall is a cage or box filled with rocks, sand, gravel, riprap or concrete. Interestingly, the lifespan of a gabion wall depends not on the strength of the rocks, but on a finer component: the wire holding them together.

The staircase ends at Montgomery; turn left. Stay left on Montgomery when Upper Drive comes in, pass an alley, Isabella Street, and take the next left onto charming Audrey Lane, a concrete alley. Like Isabella, homes on it front on either Vista or Montgomery. At its end, turn right on Patton. After passing Isabella and Audrey, it got me noticing….when a street is named for a woman, it's usually a short, relatively unimportant road. And when it happens at all, the woman's first, not last, name is used.

8 **Where Homar intersects, either stay on Patton to return to the start or keep following the directions to seldom-seen streets and a forest path (which may be muddy in wet weather). Turn right on Homar then left on Periander; at the dead-end, take the path into the woods.** This is not an official Portland Parks & Recreation trail, but a neighbor-made footpath along the side of a steep ravine. Across the ravine are homes on Upper Drive and English Lane.

Follow the path south to Portland Heights Park (ignoring side paths that descend further into the ravine), where it leads to an opening in the park's chain link fence. Enjoy the massive Oregon white oak (*quercus garryana*) in the field then climb your last 35 stairs up to the top of the park and Patton Road.

STAIRS, IN ORDER ENCOUNTERED		UP OR DOWN	NUMBER
1.	Montgomery to Greenway	Up	86
2.	Greenway to Summit	Up	36
3.	Talbot to Broadway Drive	Down	23
4.	Arden to Sherwood path	Down	8
5.	Broadway Drive to Gerald	Up	44
6.	Terrace to Broadway Drive	Down	65
7.	Broadway Drive to Davenport	Up	37
8.	Elizabeth/Terrace to Vista	Down	77
9.	Vista to Ainsworth School Annex	Down	24
10.	Ainsworth School Greenspace	Down	35
11.	Alta Vista to Montgomery	Down	59
12.	Portland Heights Park	Up	35
Total on route			529

Urban Forages for More Stairs, Hidden Paths, and Pedestrian Bridges

The book's six mapped stair walks cover 70 public staircases. These 12 adventures add another 72 staircases, 11 hidden paths, 20 bridges, and two tunnels.

Routes range from 2 to 7 miles, with one 17-mile bike loop. Because many staircases have gutters, ramps, or elevators alongside them, many of the routes are eminently bikeable.

BELOW SW KINGSTON, AT WASHINGTON PARK'S PEANUT BOWL.

Quadrant	Urban Forage	Miles	Staircases / Stairs	Hidden Paths	Bridges or Tunnels
North	Tour de Peninsula	17	6 / 300	1	6
Northeast	Rocky Butte, Rose City Park, and Siskiyou Square	6.5	5/ 250	2	1
Northwest	Mt. Calvary Cemetery, Meridian Ridge, and Skyline	2+	2 / 381	0	0
Southeast	Crystal Springs Rhododendron Garden, Reed Lake, and Bullseye Glass	3.5	6 / 204	0	2
Southeast	MAX Stairs, Springwater Trail, and Three Creeks	4.5	2 / 75	1	5
Southeast	Three Parks, Lone Fir Cemetery, and Loyola Jesuit Center	4 or 7	4 / 206	1	0
Willamette River	Two Bridges, Floating Sidewalk, and Swimming Hole	2.5	7/385	0	2
Southwest	Gander Ridge and Portland State University	3	8 / 802	2	0
Southwest	Tilikum Crossing to Marquam Hill	3	6/404	1	4
Southwest	Terwilliger Parkway to Willamette River	4 or 4.8	5 / 482	1	1
Southwest	Washington Park, Arlington Heights, and Rose Garden	4.5	9 / 809	1	0
Southwest/ Northwest	Downtown and the Pearl District	2.5 to 5	11 / 613	1	1

Bike/ped bridge between Pier and Chimney parks

Tour de Peninsula

North Portland is a peninsula between the Columbia and Willamette rivers, and is as flat as Portland gets. This 17-mile urban bike or walking loop has 250+ stairs, six pedestrian bridges, and nine parks. You'll explore the Adidas campus, descend and climb Waud Bluff, visit a lagoon, and travel scenic Willamette Blvd to Pier Park, a lesser known gem in Portland's park system. Food and drink are never far away. Mileage in parentheses is accumulated. Riding on Sundays means quiet streets on otherwise trafficky Swan Island.

Neighborhoods
BOISE, OVERLOOK, SWAN ISLAND, UNIVERSITY PARK, CATHEDRAL PARK, ARBOR LODGE, PIEDMONT, HUMBOLDT

STAIRS AND PEDESTRIAN BRIDGES

- ▪▪ Failing over I-5: 33 stairs or ramp up to bridge and 33 stairs or ramp down

- ▪▪ Concord over Going: spiral ramp and bridge

- ▪▪ Adidas campus: multiple staircases down to Greeley, or a bridge/ramp over and down to Greeley

- ▪▪ Greeley to Going, to Swan Island: 77 stairs (or bike via streets)

- ▪▪ Basin up to Willamette Blvd (Waud Bluff Trail): 48 stairs with gutter, bridge and ramp

- ▪▪ Pier Park to Chimney Park: bridge over tracks

- ▪▪ Bryant over I-5: path to bridge, both sides

- ▪▪ Peninsula Park: 18 stairs or ramp into sunken rose garden

BRYANT STREET OVERPASS

Start and end at 4.5-acre Unthank Park, 510 N Shaver Street. It's named for DeNorval Unthank, Sr., (1899-1977) one of Oregon's first black physicians and civil rights heroes. **At its south boundary, head west on Failing. Cross I-5 via the pedestrian bridge. In one block turn right on Montana, and left on Shaver; cross Interstate and in four blocks turn right on Concord. In four blocks, climb the looping ramp up and over Going Street. Descend to Pittman Addition HydroPark,** a neglected area transformed into an arty little hangout by neighbors. (To shave distance, bike through the opening in the wall, turn right on Going, and head downhill in the separated bike lane to Swan Island. Rejoin the route at the turn onto Basin Avenue.)

Go straight on Concord five blocks and turn left on Humboldt. Pass Beach Elementary School and a heritage Oregon white oak at 1815. Humboldt dead-ends at paths leading into the Adidas campus *(1.7 miles)*. Unlike Nike, Adidas lets walkers use the sidewalks and trails on its property. Explore around and descend some of the many staircases

PIER PARK POOL

or the pedestrian bridge/ramp to Greeley, the main street running through the campus. The ramp starts near the yellow building; each building is accented with a color from the Olympic rings.

Head downhill on Greeley. In 0.25 mile, at the light for Going Court, either carry your bike down the 77 steps to Going Street, or turn left at the light to hairpin down to Going, and turn right on it.

From the base of the stairs, it's 0.1 mile to Basin Street, the first right. Follow Basin 2 miles to the Waud Bluff Trail. This stretch, in the Swan Island Industrial Park, is the least scenic section; heavy freight traffic had me riding on the sidewalk. Views up the bluff from here are interesting. You are riding atop landfill. The lowlands here were known as Mock's Bottom for early settler Henry Mock who arrived in 1852. In the 1980s they were developed as the industrial park you see today, and the name changed by someone at the Port of Portland who decided "Bottom" was too suggestive. It's now called Mock's Landing.

ST. JOHNS BRIDGE FROM NEIGHBORHOOD

BIKE GUTTER ON WAUD BLUFF STAIRS TO WILLAMETTE BLVD

At the light at Emerson, turn left, then right into a parking lot, to find a small paved trail leading to the base of the Swan Island Lagoon, in the boat ramp area. The lagoon used to be the main shipping channel, when Swan Island was still a true island. 1920s dredging and fill turned the island into a peninsula. The big square maw on the left is a full-scale wind tunnel where Daimler Trucks tests truck bodies.

Continue on Basin to its dead-end at the forested base of Waud Bluff. Ascend the Waud Bluff Trail to the blufftop and Willamette Blvd. After the staircase, stop for an excellent view of ships in the lagoon. At its far end, at the downstream tip of Swan Island is a drydock operated by Vigor. It has repaired and performed maintenance on 900-foot cruise ships at its Vigorous drydock, the longest floating drydock in North America. It also builds ships there, including tugboats for Tidewater Barge Lines.

On the Waud Bluff Trail, cross over the rail tracks then climb the bluff; its sunny, well-drained location means it's great habitat for Pacific madrona, Oregon white oak, and Willamette Valley ponderosa pine. The old dirt bluff trail is still visible. The Bureau of Environmental Services cleaned up the bluff when this deluxe trail went in. New plantings are thriving.

At the top of the trail *(4.6 miles)*, turn left and follow Willamette Blvd 3 miles to Reno. Along the way, you'll pass over the deep railroad cut, dug in the early 1900s. To the left is the Railroad Bridge. Soon after, pass a vintage tavern, the Portway, from the days the waterfront at the base of the bluff was thick with heavy industry and blue-collar jobs. Further on, pass under the approaches to the St. Johns Bridge, and in nine more blocks, turn off Willamette one block from its dead-end.

Turn right on Reno. Cross Lombard at a light; in five more blocks (cutting through Sitton School's lot) turn left on James, which faces 87-acre Pier Park. Because it's so far out on the peninsula, many Portlanders have never been to this park. They're missing out. Disc golfers wandering around in its deep green, atmospheric woods are fun to watch, and the park's trails are great to explore. Its outdoor pool under the firs is a Northwest classic.

A bit to the right of the James and Reno intersection, enter the park on a paved trail. Meander around and eventually head to the park's northwest end, to find the pedestrian/bike trail over train tracks. It leads to Chimney Park *(8.7 miles).* This newish bridge is part of the 40-Mile Loop Trail System encircling the city. Stop after you cross over. Beyond the dog offleash area is Columbia Boulevard. Beyond that is the former St. Johns Landfill, the final resting place for Portland's trash from 1940 to 1990. Metro assumed responsibility for the property in 1990. Renamed St. Johns Prairie, the soil capping the landfill has been planted with native flowers; the plan, after off-gassing of methane is mostly complete, is to build trails and open it

GIANT ADIDAS SHOES GETTING A MAKEOVER FOR A VISIT BY THE WASHINGTON HUSKIES

as a park. The brick building in Chimney Park used to be the city's incinerator, and later, oddly, housed its archives.

Turn around here. Go back to Pier Park; from James (the park's south boundary) and Bruce, go straight on Bruce. In three blocks turn left on Central and go 0.8 mile to the 6-acre St. Johns Community Center and Park. Big London plane trees (*Platanus* x *acerifolia*) are a highlight. This building was a daycare during WWII for workers in the St. Johns shipyards.

Keep on Central another 0.7 mile to Roosevelt High School *(11 miles)*. Check out the new remodel, which turned a 96-year-old building into a digital era showpiece.

At Roosevelt's east end, turn right on Ida; in one block come to Lombard and turn left. Cross over the railroad cut; in three blocks turn right on Westanna. Pass 4.5-acre McKenna Park.

A few blocks past the park, go left on Yale. Pass cute Astor School. At Yale's end, turn right on Olin, immediately left on Harvard, and you're back at the top of the Waud Bluff Trail. Turn left on Willamette Blvd and ride its bike lane. Enjoy the far-ranging views, of Swan Island, downtown, and Forest Park.

Pass a panhandle of Columbia Park (with restroom) called Columbia Annex. Next to the park is an 1891 Queen Anne built by John Mock, son of Henry Mock who lived in the bottomlands you crossed earlier. John settled here and the area is still known as Mock's Crest.

After another 0.5 mile on Willamette, watch for Wabash on the left (look for a painted cross walk). Turn left on it and instantly right on Bryant. Take Bryant 0.6 mile to Arbor Lodge Park *(14 miles)*, on the right, with its innovative, all-ability Harper's Playground. A block to the north, a green fir island betrays the location of tiny, beautiful Gammans Park.

Stay on Bryant; cross Interstate and MAX tracks at a crosswalk; jog left to stay east on Bryant and enjoy one of the city's unpaved blocks. Turn right on Montana and left on Saratoga. A freeway wall looks like a dead-end, but pass through a portal to another pedestrian/bike bridge. Cross over and continue east on Bryant.

In one block turn right on Michigan. Cross Rosa Parks Way at the crosswalk and turn left; in two blocks you're at Peninsula Park. *(15.7 miles)* Explore this 16-acre park. It's one of the prettiest, most formal city parks in town. Stop to see the fantastic murals in the 1913 community center. It was designed by Ellis Lawrence, architect of the elegant Title Wave Bookstore not far from here. He founded University of Oregon's school of architecture.

Don't miss the sunken rose garden at the south end. Descend the stairs (or a ramp) and meander its paths. This whole park, while formal and symmetric, has a wonderful mix of spaces and ways to enjoy it. It's a product of the City Beautiful movement of the early 1900s, during which elegant urban parks were thought to inspire city residents to moral and civic virtue. It's a good example of what cities can do best: create beautiful places for fun, community, and peaceful contemplation.

Leave the park at its south boundary, Ainsworth, and head south on Kerby. Pass through Portland Community College's Cascade campus, cross Killingsworth, then pass Jefferson High on the left (riding the sidewalk a few blocks where Kerby turns one-way). At Prescott, jog left to stay on Kerby and return to the start.

Rocky Butte, Rose City Park, and Siskiyou Square

At 612 feet, and with nearly 360-degree views, Rocky Butte is Portland's most scenic overlook. On a clear day you can see east to Crown Point in the Columbia Gorge, and west to the St. Johns Bridge. Volcanic peaks, downtown, jets landing at PDX: it's got it all. At the butte's top is a Depression-era masterpiece of stonework, with hand-tooled basalt stairs and rock walls. The butte top and its approach roads are preserved as the Rocky Butte Scenic Drive Historic District, on the National Register of Historic Places.

The butte is the eroded plug of a volcano. During the Missoula Floods, floodwaters roared out of the tight confines of the Gorge and smashed into Rocky Butte's east face, shearing it nearly vertical. Along its south and west sides, scour channels formed, depressions left by the water as it churned in, then drained out.

On the way to top of the butte, this 6.5-mile stair walk explores parts of that scour channel, now occupied by parks and neighborhoods. The route gains and loses about 400 feet of elevation.

Neighborhoods
ROSEWAY, ROSE CITY PARK, MADISON SOUTH, ROCKY BUTTE HISTORIC DISTRICT

STAIRS AND HIDDEN PATHS

- Sacramento and 62nd into Rose City Park: 67 stairs
- Rocky Butte's grand staircase: 72 stairs
- Rocky Butte's hidden path and staircase: 33 stairs to a path to a tunnel
- Hidden path at the end of Russell Place
- Stairs in Siskiyou Square: various
- Madison High School, to 82nd: 47 stairs

SOUTHEAST VIEW ATOP ROCKY BUTTE

Begin at Glenhaven Park, 7900 NE Siskiyou Street. Walk to its southwest corner (tennis courts), and on to the dead-end of Alameda. Walk out Alameda two blocks, then left onto Sacramento.

This beautiful road sits above the flood-scoured depression that is home to Rose City Park. After 70th are fantastic views to the south.

At 62nd, descend stairs into the park, and take the path along the golf course fence, heading southeast to Tillamook. Turn left on Tillamook, stopping at 72nd in the park's historic clubhouse for a snack or restroom break. Stay on Tillamook, then turn left on 88th. In five blocks cross Russell Street. In one more block turn right on Russell Place, which sits on the slopes of a dramatic, bowl-like scoured area. In one block, turn left on Fremont Drive, and then quick right on 89th, which climbs out of the bowl. After one long block, turn right on Hill Way, cross 92nd and turn immediately left on Cadet, which starts inauspiciously but gets better. I would wager that 99.9 percent of Portlanders have never

ROSE CITY PARK GOLF CLUBHOUSE

been on this street. Both "Hill Way" and "Cadet" come from the butte's days as the Hill Military Academy. The academy's grounds, including fortresslike dorms complete with crenellated tops, are now owned by City Bible Church, a large evangelical Christian church. The dorms are inhabited by students at Portland Bible College, a ministry of the church.

Cadet ends at Fremont. The property on the right, including Fremont, is owned by the church. So turn left on Fremont, then immediately right on 91st, which curves around the church's vast parking lot. The domes that look like they might be storing rock salt are its sanctuary. Follow the road uphill, and enjoy the WPA (Works Projects Administration) stonework along the way. You'll pass over a pedestrian tunnel that leads to a trail. Cadets at the military academy passed through that tunnel with their livestock, pasturing the animals in the valley now occupied by I-205. In those years, Rocky Butte was a major auto-touring attraction and the road a hazard to livestock, hence the tunnel.

Walk to the top, to Joseph Wood Hill Park. This WPA project offered men left unemployed by the Depression an opportunity for meaningful work. The mostly unskilled men were taught to work the stone by experts—the men who had created the stonework of the Historic Columbia River Highway in the Gorge in the 1910s. The park at the butte's summit is named for the founder of the military academy.

After enjoying the views, walk to the summit's north end and descend the formal staircase. Turn left, walking along a magnificent ashlar wall (i.e., rough stone hand-cut to create a rustic, irregular surface). Stop at the first intersection: this is the top of the butte's south approach road. Like the north approach, it's also called Rocky Butte Road.

ROCKY BUTTE'S 375-FOOT, CURVING TUNNEL

Pick option 1 or 2 here:

1. Descend steep railroad-tie steps to a trail at the base of a tall stone wall. Walk its length and just before the trail climbs back to the road, turn right on a dirt path. It's a steep downhill, not for creaky knees. Portland Parks has done wonderful work removing invasives here and, in 2017, topping or cutting trees to maintain views from the top. You'll see evidence of that. At a trail junction, turn left and soon arrive at the upper portal of the butte's 375-foot, switchbacking tunnel. Turn left and walk the tunnel's sidewalk.

2. Or… forego the steep trail. Instead, from the top, turn right on the south approach road and walk its length to the tunnel. You'll walk through the tunnel this way as well.

After emerging from the tunnel, cross the saddle of the butte, low enough that floodwaters poured over it. Keep on until Rocky Butte Road ends at Russell and 92nd. Walk west on Russell. Turn right on 88th and in one block, left on Russell Place. Continue, at its dead-end, onto a hidden path into 14-acre Siskiyou Square. On the right, the fenced area is a wetland at the bottom of the flood-scoured depression seen earlier. After a child drowned here years ago, the fence went up.

The land you're entering is owned by Dharma Rain Zen Center. It offers instruction in Zen practice and Buddhist teachings. This fascinating place occupies the old Rose City Sand and Gravel quarry, where flood deposits were mined from about 1936 to 1972. After that, for 10 years construction debris and organic and volatile materials were landfilled here, filling the 80-foot pit. You may see pipes installed to vent the resulting methane. From 1982 on, the site was left fallow, a brownfield with environmental hazards. At one point, Walmart wanted to build here, but the neighborhood association objected. It retreated but generously offered its environmental investigations to the new owners.

In 2012 the Buddhist community, then based in Buckman, purchased the land, and is in early stages of restoring and regenerating it as an Oregon white oak savanna, a meditation center, and co-housing community. Dharma Rain has many partners whose grants and expertise are helping make its vision reality. Bureau of Environment Services, Metro, Friends of Trees, and East Multnomah Soil and Water Conservation District are a few. The largest building you'll see is a Sodo, or meditation hall. A covered walkway around it is for walking meditation.

Follow the path to 82nd. At Siskiyou, cross 82nd at the stoplight to return to Glenhaven Park. Or turn left and cross 82nd at the light at Madison High School. A staircase at its south end elevates you to great views of the butte and its saddle. Imagine this scene 15,000 years ago: everything below that saddle was under water.

WPA HAND-TOOLED ROCKWORK ON ROCKY BUTTE ROAD

MERIDIAN RIDGE STAIRS

Mt. Calvary Cemetery, Meridian Ridge, and Skyline

Save this stair walk for a crystal-clear day; the four-volcano views are spectacular. Highlights are a visit to one of Portland's most beautiful cemeteries and two magnificent staircases. The hilly route is about 2 miles, or more if you explore the cemetery. Its staircase climbs to one of the city's highest peaks, at 1,070 feet. Cemetery grounds between Burnside and Barnes roads are especially beautiful, with old headstones and trees, a memorial to the Irish Famine, and a heartbreaking children's section.

Neighborhoods
SYLVAN HIGHLANDS, FOREST PARK

STAIRS

- ▪▪ Mt. Calvary Cemetery: 107 stairs, traveled both ways

- ▪▪ Meridian Ridge neighborhood: 167 stairs

Dogs, Caution, Parking: No dogs are allowed on the cemetery grounds. Skyline Blvd, which you walk briefly between sites, is not ideal for walking. It's curvy, has an on-again-off-again shoulder, and cars travel fast. Where there's no shoulder, walk single-file facing traffic. Bikes are common on Skyline, so watch for them too. If you drive, don't park in the cemetery lot because you'll be exploring beyond the cemetery. Drive a short bit beyond it. On Skyline, just north of where it splits from Burnside is a small manicured bit of cemetery surrounded by trees; park on either side of Skyline here. Walk back to the start via the cemetery road that starts about 100 feet south.

Start at TriMet's bus 20 stop at Mt. Calvary Cemetery (333 SW Skyline). It's next to the stone cemetery office building. The Catholic Archdiocese bought this land in 1888, after its first cemetery was filled at what is now Central Catholic High School in Southeast Portland. (That land had been donated to the Church in 1858 by Timothy Sullivan, of Sullivan's Gulch). In the 1930s, about 2,000 human remains from that site were relocated here. The office building is faced with basalt quarried at Rocky Butte.

Across Skyline, begin climbing a gorgeous landscape staircase to an altar under a stone baldachin (a ceremonial canopy over an altar or throne). The stairs, altar and baldachin date from the 1930s. Beyond the altar, climb to the top of the peak and a beautiful Art Deco mausoleum

MAUSOLEUM AT MT. CALVARY SUMMIT

VIEWS OF CASCADE PEAKS ABOVE MERIDIAN RIDGE

from the 1940s. Views are fantastic, the more so for the solitude and beauty at this peak.

When you're done at the peak, descend the stairs. From the bottom, walk the cemetery road west to Skyline and continue west (right). Much of the 0.2-mile distance can be walked on grassy areas off the road and along two more sections of Mt. Calvary's graves. Walk into these subsections: views are beautiful and stone benches invite you to enjoy them. As you walk Skyline, the land to your left is also owned by the Archdiocese; it was planned for cemetery expansion, but with fewer people wanting burial, the plans seem to be shelved for now.

From Skyline, turn right on Royal Blvd and walk downhill. Turn left on Meridian Ridge Drive and you'll soon see the start of the epic staircase. Its 167 stairs up to Skyline pass by enormous new homes. The radio towers above were built in 2000 on a small peak; the taller one is 282 feet tall. At the top of the steps, views are wonderful: the green forest of the Audubon sanctuaries and beyond, Cascade volcanoes.

From the stairs, turn left on Skyline, and walk the shoulder 0.2 mile to Willamette Stone State Heritage Site (253 NW Skyline). Learn online before you go about our national system of surveying land, a vital element in the manifest destiny philosophy that held we Americans were destined to expand, claim, and develop across North America, due to our special virtues. More practically, every time you buy or sell real property, your deed has a property description based on this national survey system.

Return to the start via Skyline. Since you're up on Skyline Ridge, get a bite at the Skyline Restaurant, 1313 NW Skyline Blvd. It's been there since 1935. Or for a local beer, great sandwiches and killer views, go a bit further to the Skyline Tavern, 8031 NW Skyline. If the weather is fine, that's definitely the better choice; sit outside overlooking the Tualatin Valley, throw some horseshoes and enjoy the life you're living.

Stairs ascending Mt. Calvary

Portland firefighters on steps at SE Bybee MAX station, in training mode

Crystal Springs Rhododendron Garden, Reed Lake, and Bullseye Glass

This stair walk isn't too long—just 3.5 miles—but has intriguing side adventures that are destinations on their own. The walk starts and ends at two Orange Line MAX stations. Do it in spring when the rhododendron garden is at its peak. Mothers Day is generally the apex of bloom.

Dogs must be leashed in the garden, Reed Canyon, and on the Reed campus.

STAIRS AND PEDESTRIAN BRIDGES

- ▪▪ SE Bybee Blvd MAX station: 51 stairs or elevator

- ▪▪ Crystal Springs Rhododendron Garden: 23 stairs to the creek; plus other staircases

- ▪▪ Reed Canyon: pedestrian bridge across Reed Lake

- ▪▪ Kenilworth Park: 19 stairs

- ▪▪ Grout School to 31st: 18 stairs

- ▪▪ Lafayette to Rhone stairs/bridge over tracks: 45 up and 48 down, or elevator

PEDESTRIAN BRIDGE OVER REED LAKE

ON THE REED COLLEGE CAMPUS

Begin at the SE Bybee Blvd MAX station. Glass mosaics on the posts here evoke the flowers of the rhododendron garden you'll soon pass through. The glass was manufactured at Bullseye Glass, another stop on this urban forage. The art in the cupola in the tower is three layers of glass that are painted, etched, screen-printed, and laminated together. It was inspired by nearby Crystal Springs Creek.

Climb its stairs and turn left on Bybee. Pass the clubhouse for the century-old Eastmoreland Golf Course. It's open to nongolfers should you want a refreshment of the adult beverage sort or otherwise. Enjoy the giant sequoias on your left. On your right are the grand homes of Eastmoreland.

As Bybee curves north it becomes 28th. At Woodstock Blvd, stay on 28th. Tour Crystal Springs Rhododendron Garden, 9.5 acres of spring-fed creeks, waterfalls, a lake, and mature rhodies blooming early March into June. Hard to believe that in the 1940s this exquisite place was covered in blackberries and weeds. See Portland Parks' website for when, and for whom, it's free to enter.

Exit the gardens, cross 28th, and enter Reed College via its west portal. Take a photo of the campus map here. Walk, either directly or meanderingly, over to the grandeur of Eliot Hall. You'll pass the Old Dorm Block, which looks like no dorm I ever inhabited. Have questions about a tree on Reed's arboretumlike campus? For a location-based description, visit reed.edu and search for *trees*.

From Eliot Hall, walk north, crossing Reed Lake on a pedestrian bridge. You may want to do the 0.8-mile hike that encircles the lake and crosses some of the eponymous springs in Crystal Springs Creek, Lake, and Rhododendron Garden. The canyon trail is on the Reed map; or find a more detailed map at Reed.edu/canyon. The hike is lovely; the canyon is one of Portland's great natural treasures, with its pristine springs, and forest that has been stripped of the non-native invasives that once colonized it.

Once across Reed Lake, walk north, aiming to leave the campus at 33rd and Steele. I encountered a swing set on my path.

At Steele, go right one block to 34th and turn left. In four blocks, cross Holgate with care and enter Kenilworth Park. Diagonal left under tall firs through this exceptionally pretty park. Head to a low red-brick wall around a patio that offers a nice view of OHSU's campus on Marquam Hill. Descend stairs next to the wall. It turns out the patio is the roof of a lovely, but dilapidated park structure with a classical Italian colonnade.

Exit the park and walk west on the paved area between Grout School and its playground. Descend stairs to 31st and turn right. Walk half a block and turn left on Cora, which has that good old "roadway not improved" vibe. Stay on it, heading downhill toward former wetlands now industrial land and rail yards.

Turn right at 24ᵗʰ, and in one block, left on Gladstone. Fred Meyer's headquarters is the vast office building on your right.

Turn right on 22ⁿᵈ, and here's a nice place to eat, Lunchbox Café in the Freddy's building. You don't need an employee badge to go in. There's something very meta about eating here.

Turn left on Bush and pass Bullseye Glass, which sometimes emits enticing tinkling sounds. Check out the tank of minus 360-degree cryogenic oxygen. When combined with natural gas, used in glass production, the oxygen reduces both fuel consumption and greenhouse gases, says the sign explaining how harmless the alarming looking pipes are. On a 35-degree day, they were covered in what looked like glacial snowpack.

Turn right on 21st and go into Bullseye's Resource Center, where you can buy glass, supplies, or just marvel at the beautiful art glass for sale. Is there anything to buy for those of us who are mere appreciators? Yes! Check out the mold samples (way more beautiful than they sound) and bags and tee shirts. Displays show how glass is made, the sheets of art glass are seductive, and a gallery upstairs shows some of the work artists have created with Bullseye's glass. It's a homegrown company that was at the forefront of Portland's current creative renaissance, when it began in 1974.

From 21st, turn left on Lafayette and in one block come to the shiny new stairs/bridge that cross the rail tracks. Beautiful, but I do miss the "will-this-thing-collapse" wooden stairs and bridge that it replaced.

Come down the stairs and you're on Rhine. The SE 17ᵗʰ and Rhine MAX station is one block away, at route's end. The weathered steel rowboats along the station were inspired by the waterway that once cut through the land here, a long-ago channel of the Willamette River. Plants surround them like waves.

WPA-ERA ROCKWORK AND WATERFALL ON JOHNSON CREEK

MAX Stairs, Springwater Trail, and Three Creeks

This 4.5-mile MAX-to-MAX station walk has two staircases bookending three creeks and pedestrian/bike bridges. Most wonderfully, it also goes out onto an island. Most of Portland's urban creeks run underground in pipes. These are exceptions. Despite their troubles, they are beautiful, and the focus of ongoing work to restore their health and habitats.

Neighborhoods
SELLWOOD, ARDENWALD-JOHNSON CREEK, WOODSTOCK, EASTMORELAND

STAIRS, PEDESTRIAN/CYCLIST BRIDGES, AND CREEKS

- ▪▪ SE Tacoma/Johnson Creek MAX station: wetland boardwalk and 24 stairs or ramp
- ▪▪ Bridges over Johnson Creek, McLoughlin Blvd and Union Pacific tracks
- ▪▪ Crystal Springs Creek and Errol Creek
- ▪▪ SE Bybee Blvd MAX station: 51 stairs or elevator

Start at the SE Tacoma/Johnson Creek MAX station. If you drive, park free in the Park and Ride, but it fills up early on weekdays. The glass-mosaic poles are homage to the fish in Johnson Creek. The giant circles, entitled "Kerf," are pigmented concrete and dirt. They are earth casts: molds are carved into the dirt and the concrete poured into them. They pay homage to the water wheels that powered woolen mills and saw mills here.

Enjoy the interpretive boardwalk over Johnson Creek's wetlands, ending at the creek. The walk honors Roy and Wilma Bishop, whose Oregon Worsted Mill was on this site. They are part of the same family that owns Pendleton Woolen Mills. Oregon Worsted began in 1918 making uniforms at the US Army's request. The company, still family-operated, evolved into the Mill End Store, which moved because of construction of this project. It's now a mile away, at 9701 SE McLoughlin, in Milwaukie.

Here you're near the end of Johnson Creek's 26-mile run, which starts near Boring, Oregon. Native Americans lived along it and early settlers began taming it. First came small dams in the 1840s, then rail lines (one of which you'll be soon walking on), then 14 miles of channelization in the 1930s by WPA crews, in what ultimately was an unsuccessful flood control effort.

Since the 1990s, some of the human changes to the floodplain have been deconstructed, with agencies in the Johnson Creek Conservation Partnership buying land from willing sellers. Their goals include ripping out impervious surfaces (cement, roofs, asphalt) and allowing the creek to return to wetlands and shallow side channels needed by salmon species. In the process they are eliminating insurance claims to rebuild flooded structures when the creek floods again.

Climb stairs to Tenino and turn left. Cross ramps to McLoughlin, then turn left on 21st, where, so charmingly, Crystal Springs Creek runs along the street. It's a 2.7-mile, spring-fed creek that originates in Reed Canyon. It's one of two spring-fed creeks on the route, both tributaries of Johnson Creek. The Brannen property, public land at 21st and Umatilla, is where a garage once straddled the creek and a culvert blocked fish passage; now it's a small natural area with the creek running on the surface. With removal of seven fish-blocking culverts in the early 2000s, steelhead, lamprey and coho salmon again swim in Crystal Springs Creek. Its year-round, even flow of cold water is ideal habitat for salmon.

From 21st, turn left on Sherrett and then quickly right at a split rail fence that leads to a peninsula: Crystal Springs Creek on your right; Johnson Creek on your left. Their confluence is just beyond. A house used to occupy this peninsula.

Cross the bridge over Crystal Springs Creek, and walk to 21st. Turn left on 21st, right on Marion, and left on 19th to a Springwater Trail trailhead. Turn left, toward Powell Butte.

The first bridge crosses Johnson Creek. The next crosses over McLoughlin Boulevard. Its steel arch is a gateway between Portland and Milwaukie for drivers.

After the McLoughlin bridge, exit the trail for a side trip to a historic building and business, the Pendleton Woolen Mill Store. Once a working woolen mill called the Foundation Mill, it sells Pendleton fabrics and products made in Washougal, Washington or Pendleton, Oregon. More intriguing are mysterious detritus from the mill such as wool slugs, wool worms, scrap strips, and selvage. People, it seems, make stuff with all of them.

Back on the Springwater Trail, cross the third bridge over MAX and Union Pacific tracks. After the tracks, East Side Plating is on the left. Since 1946, this shop has provided metal finishes such as anodizing and powder coating, or laser marking of parts. It's an example of the heavy industry that also calls the Johnson Creek floodplain its home.

The trail's prior life as a rail alignment is quite apparent here. Cross under 32nd. Next, the trail crosses Johnson Creek, entering Tideman Johnson Natural Area, a never-developed bottomland. Explore its side trail, which loops back to the main trail.

Cross Johnson Creek again, and 100 feet or so beyond the bridge, look left for a side trail; it leads to an interesting view of the downstream tip of the island you'll soon be on. Johnson Creek flows around the island, and its banks here show the WPA rockwork and man-made waterfall that armored the creek into a channel. The City owns the land between the creek and the Springwater Trail so you can walk east on the parallel dirt path or the trail itself to 45th.

Turn left off the Springwater Trail at 45th. Restroom here. Just east of where you're turning off, the trail passes a large industrial inhabitant of the floodplain, Precision Castparts. One of Oregon's

SE Tacoma/Johnson Creek MAX station

Along Crystal Springs Creek

three Fortune 500 companies, it makes parts primarily for the aerospace industry.

Walk north on 45th. Find coffee and a food mart, along with a Franz Bakery outlet. Keep left at the Y where 45th Place veers right.

To walk onto the rare island-in-the-city, **turn left on Harney.** Once over the tiny bridge, you're on it. Since the 1996 floods walloped Johnson Creek, the City of Portland has worked to buy available parcels in the floodplain. It owns one of the seven houses on this island. At the dead-end, the island's downstream tip, you can stand atop the viewpoint created by WPA crews.

Come back out of the dead-end; just past the bridge, turn left at an opening in a fenced area, the Errol Creek Confluence Restoration Project. This land acquisition is aimed at recreating off-channel habitat, removing invasives, and reconnecting Errol Creek to its floodplain. Errol Creek flows into Johnson Creek near here. Walk the path north to the next street, Umatilla. In winter 2018, a decayed house built in 1915, on the right, was boarded up. Owned by the City, its days appeared to be numbered. Keep straight on gravel 44th to Tenino. A spring emerges from the yard at 4401, runs along the street and then flows into the creek.

Walk east on Tenino, turn left on 45th, and take the first left onto Crystal Springs Blvd. Walk this exceptionally pretty street all the way back. You may want to investigate dead ends of Cesar Chavez and off it, Berkeley Way. Interesting. West of about 36th on the boulevard, homes and lots are huge and elegant, ready for a *Sunset* magazine photo shoot. After 30th, on the left Eastmoreland Golf Course, part of Portland Parks & Recreation, is essentially a private park just for golfers. Enjoy the trees, but from a distance.

Keep on Crystal Springs Blvd as it curves north and becomes 27th. At Bybee turn left and walk stairs down to the MAX station.

Springwater emerging from a yard, flowing toward Johnson Creek

Beech grove at Creston Park

Three Parks, Lone Fir Cemetery, and Loyola Jesuit Center

This 4-mile one-way stair walk with bus return (or 7-mile loop) explores three lovely Southeast Portland parks, with a pass through Lone Fir, Portland's most historic cemetery/arboretum. Near the end, visit a 90-year old plant nursery and the Loyola Jesuit Center's serene trail under very tall trees. Portland's rich horticultural heritage is on display on this loop.

Before your walk, read up on the cemetery's history at friendsoflonefircemetery.org. Plan to have lunch along the way; you're never far from great food in Southeast Portland. This is an ideal autumn walk, for leaf color in the cemetery and parks.

No dogs are allowed at Lone Fir, and no bikes or dogs are allowed on the Loyola Jesuit Center path.

STAIRS

- **Colonel Summers Park** from 18th and Belmont into the park: 23 stairs

- **Laurelhurst Park** next to 3360 SE Ankeny into the park: 88 stairs

- **Creston Park** from 43rd and Powell into the park: 35 stairs

- **Creston Park** from the swimming pool to the terrace above: 60 stairs

Southeast Portland is part of the Portland Basin, river sediments up to 1,800 feet deep deposited from millions of years ago to the last Ice Age. Here, erosion of the sediments has created a series of broad terraces stair-stepping up from the Willamette River.

Start on Belmont and 18th. Walk to 18th's dead-end, and descend stairs into small Colonel Summers Park. It got lots of love in 2017 from Portland's latest parks bond measure, approved by voters to do long-deferred park maintenance. The old picnic enclosure now has beautiful laser-cut steel panels, and a Portland Loo and splash pad have been installed. The Loo, a toilet kiosk, is open mid-March to mid-November. Loo gets a capital *L* because it's a trademarked, patented invention, made in Portland's Guild's Lake Industrial Sanctuary. No matter where Loos go, from Texas to British Columbia, they are Portland Loos. They even have their own website.

A community garden at the park's east end is one of 52 gardens the City manages. Plots range from ADA-accessible, to "starter" size, to quad plots for serious canners. Annual rent ranges from $15 to $200.

If the gate is unlocked, one of the gardeners is there, and you can go in. Otherwise it's locked to prevent predation.

A potential gardener applies via an online application. If a space is available, they can begin. The City provides water, compost, and coffee bags (for putting your plot to bed in the winter—they prevent weed growth). In return, each gardener commits to six hours per year of service for general garden upkeep. Part of this garden's produce is "Produce for People," i.e., greens, onions, and tomatoes donated to food pantries. Each garden has a volunteer manager or two.

From the park, head north on 20th to Lone Fir Cemetery. Enter at 21st and Morrison. Gravestones are fascinating, but so are the trees—700 trees representing 67 different species. The eponymous fir, which was the only tree on the property in the 1850s, has an identifying plaque. It's near the northwest corner, in view of Stark Street. Emmor Stephens was the first person buried here, interred on his son's property in 1846, nine years before the land became a cemetery. I love the Woodmen of the World graves—concrete, ivy-covered tree stumps. The men buried under them were members of a fraternal organization, in the days before virtual friendships.

By the 1920s the cemetery had become neglected, and was covered in blackberries, making its current state of beauty even more remarkable. Come back for a guided tour; find dates at Friends of Lone Fir Cemetery's website. They also host headstone-cleaning parties and other esoteric forms of civic engagement.

Meander through the cemetery to the east entrance on 26th. Turn left on 26th, right on Stark, left on 28th (food options here) and right on Ankeny. At 33rd and Ankeny, two of the city's grandest mansions are perched on a rise above Laurelhurst Park. The exuberant and eclectic 3316 was designed in 1928 by Herman Brookman, architect of the equally grand Temple Beth Israel in

Northwest Portland. Next door is a red brick home built in 1912 by soon-to-be Portland mayor H. Russell Albee. The public staircase is just east of it. The stairs match the mansion, and I suspect they were a little perk the mayor requested of city crews. His home's construction was about the same time that 31-acre Laurelhurst Park was acquired and developed by the City's park superintendent Emanuel Mische. He had earlier worked for the famous Olmsted Brothers landscape architecture firm. That firm's emphasis on naturalistic landscaping is reflected in Laurelhurst Park's winding paths and the vistas that open up as you walk them.

Descend the staircase from Ankeny through century-old rhododendrons to paths under tall firs and specimen trees. Loop around the trails—don't miss the south border path, which is especially lovely.

Ultimately head to the park's southeast entrance at Cesar Chavez and Stark —the safest place to cross busy Cesar Chavez. **Cross here then walk back north (left) to Oak Street (not Oak Court which is an alley). Turn right on Oak.** It's quiet and pretty. The homes on the right look different. Why? Because no driveways. They use the alley in back. The drivewayless side of Oak is much more parklike.

Turn right on 44th, left on Stark, and right on 45th. Here is Belmont Station, one of the best places to go to try a beer you've never heard of before. After your beer or kombucha or whatnot, walk south on 45th, which I've deemed a block of high interest. Cross Belmont; more food is here, on the corner. Around where Salmon crosses you begin to see a tree island ahead. That's the giant sequoias and firs at the Loyola Jesuit Center, your next destination.

Still on 45th, cross Hawthorne and walk another really nice block of creative homeownership. Cross Division, and at Woodward, 45th ends. Turn right, then left on 43rd. Walk into the forest at the Jesuit Center, at 3220. The path is to the left just beyond the iron gate. At the trail junction, turn right if you want to walk the Stations of the Cross in order. The stations offer Christians a contemplative structure for prayer as they follow Jesus's journey to his crucifixion.

After your walk in the forest, don't miss two Portland Heritage Trees. If it's late summer you're in for a show: from 43rd walk west on Franklin to Van Veen Nursery. Past its entrance, inside the fence are two crepe myrtles (*Lagerstroemia*). Their multiple trunks, smooth-barked and patchy, are almost as interesting as their riotous blooms. They're native to South Asia, and their species name derives not from an Asian, but from Magnus von Lagerström, a Swede who worked in India in the 1700s. He supplied plants to Carl Linnaeus, who formalized the biological nomenclature we use today.

Van Veen Nursery is a third-generation family business, at this location since 1926. It's primarily mail order, growing and selling rhododendrons. Rhodies bloom in old greenhouses from January to June. If you want to look around and see 80-year-old specimens, call first (503.777.1734) and they'll be glad to give you a tour.

Next up is Creston Park. Walk south on 43rd. Cross Powell at the light and turn left. You could take a path down into the park, which sits in a bowl, or go a bit further to a staircase. Once down in the park, do you see the stairs next to the swimming pool? Climb them; on the hill to your left is a fine little forest of beech trees. In fall their foliage is beautiful, and their tiny beechnuts very cute. They also have a smooth bark that has inspired people across the centuries to express themselves. But now that we have Instagram, there's no need to incise our initials into tree bark for posterity.

To return via bus to Colonel Summers Park, walk to Haig Street (one block north of Powell). At 50th and Haig (stop 7656), take TriMet's 14 bus, Hawthorne to Portland. Get off at 16th and Hawthorne and walk about 0.3 miles north back to Colonel Summers Park. Or catch the 19 bus at 43rd and Powell; it goes downtown. Or walk back any way that suits you; you'll find places to eat along Division and Hawthorne.

MANSION ON SE ANKENY STREET

Two Bridges, Floating Sidewalk, & Swimming Hole

Not many people do this approximately 2.5-mile loop with 385 stairs. Most walk the similar-length Hawthorne-Steel Bridge loop. Do this stair walk on a weekend, and end at the Portland Saturday Market. Do it in the summer and jump in the river.

STAIRS AND PEDESTRIAN BRIDGES

- Union Station bridge over rail yards: 42 stairs up, 44 stairs down, or elevator
- SW Naito Parkway to Broadway Bridge: 81 stairs
- Broadway Bridge to N Interstate Avenue: 37 stairs
- N Oregon Street to Vera Katz Eastbank Esplanade: 65 stairs or ramp
- Esplanade to Burnside Bridge: 86 stairs
- Burnside Bridge to SW 1st Avenue: 30 stairs

BROADWAY BRIDGE AND EAST SIDE STAIRCASE

Begin at the Union Station MAX station. On Irving between 5th and 6th, climb to the pedestrian bridge over the rail yards. From the bridge, look down at what used to be Couch Lake. Fifteen feet deep and about 22 city blocks in size, it was one of several bottomland lakes alongside the Willamette. In the 1880s, the Northern Pacific Terminal Company bought the land and began filling the lake with ballast from incoming ships and sand from the riverbed. It was gone by the time Union Station opened in 1896.

Once across, descend 18 stairs, keep straight, descend 26 more to Naito Parkway, and turn left. Climb 81 stairs to Broadway Bridge's sidewalk, and enjoy its commodiousness. Once across the river, descend 37 stairs to Interstate Avenue's southbound sidewalk and walk south. Pass Veterans Memorial Coliseum, a 1960 creation in the International style. Its giant concrete bowl sits inside glass walls. Threatened with demolition in 2009, it is now listed on the National Register of Historic Places. The Beatles played; the Dalai Lama spoke, and Obama stumped there.

On the right is the Louis Dreyfus Commodities O Dock, a grain elevator built in 1914. Northwest-grown grain is loaded on ships for export to Asia.

Cross Multnomah, which leads to the Steel Bridge. Keep on Interstate another 0.1 mile; cross Oregon, walk around a landscaped circle, and you'll see a staircase. Descend 11 stairs, go straight, cross over railroad tracks, descend 54 stairs, and turn left onto the Vera Katz Eastbank Esplanade. Katz (1933 to 2017) was the first woman to be the Speaker of Oregon's House of Representatives. A civil rights and public transportation leader, she served three terms as Speaker and three terms as Portland's mayor (1993-2005). She dreamed big: wanting to cap the I-405 freeway and build neighborhoods atop it (hasn't happened) and a waterfront trail on the no-man's-land that was the Willamette's east bank (you're on it).

To the right is the Steel Bridge, a photogenic study in angles and lines. The next bridge upstream is your exit: the Burnside. Walk under a freeway ramp with a truncated roadbed, an exit that never made it past the planning stage. Then walk onto the water on the floating sidewalk. Go further out on the Kevin J. Duckworth Dock, originally intended for motorized boats, but in 2017 plans were announced to reincarnate it as an urban swimming hole.

Walk under the aged Burnside Bridge, leave the floating walk and do a U-turn to a staircase climbing to the Burnside. Climb 86 steps to the sidewalk, and while crossing the river, take the obligatory photo of the White Stag sign.

At the Saturday Market/Old Town arch, descend 30 stairs to the Skidmore Fountain MAX station. If it's Saturday or Sunday, March through Christmas Eve, explore the nation's oldest, continually operating open-air crafts market. Vendors must make the items they sell, and products are juried, ensuring high quality, craftsmanship, and creativity. There are many longtime vendors, but each month a dozen or so new vendors come to the market.

To return to the start, walk north on 1st or other streets through Old Town.

PEDESTRIAN BRIDGE OVER TRAIN TRACKS, AT SITE OF COUCH LAKE

THE EPIC ELEVATOR STAIRS

Gander Ridge and Portland State University

The front half of this 3-mile stair walk clings to the flanks of the West Hills and is all about the stairs—802 of them. The turnaround is a stop on the PSU campus for lunch at a fifth-floor rooftop terrace adjacent to the Portland Archives. The return is a straightaway along innovative Montgomery Street and the Ho Chi Minh Trail.

Walk this on a Saturday, when the Portland Farmers Market turns the South Park Blocks in the PSU campus into food-lover heaven. Plan also to spend time investigating PSU's library (and its enormous beech tree), community center, urban plazas, and bookstore. The loop gains and loses about 625 feet in elevation.

STAIRS AND HIDDEN PATHS

- ▪▪ 20th to Market Street Drive: 82 stairs

- ▪▪ 16th Avenue cordonata, Montgomery to Harrison: 25

- ▪▪ 16th down to Harrison: 32

- ▪▪ Market Street Drive to Mill Street Terrace: 152

- ▪▪ 13th, between College's two levels: 69

- ▪▪ Cardinell at 12th to upper Cardinell: 182

- ▪▪ Cardinell to 10th dead-end (optional): 57

- ▪▪ Hoffman to Broadway Drive: 203

- ▪▪ Two hidden paths: the Ho Chi Minh Trail and Cardinell to Hoffman

SALMON CYCLE SCULPTURE AT PSU

Begin at the Goose Hollow/SW Jefferson Street MAX station.
Benches are planks to honor Jefferson's role in the famous Great
Plank Road that ran from Portland's docks, into the canyon west
of here, and downhill into the Tualatin Valley. Built in the early
1850s, the Plank Road was the first relatively good road over the
Tualatin Mountains into the valley. Goose Hollow is lowland along
now-buried Tanner Creek, after it flowed out of the canyon. Gander
Ridge is the hillside above Goose Hollow.

Walk west on Jefferson and turn left on 20th. On the right, pass
two Portland Heritage Trees and the Kamm Mansion, an 1871 home
originally on the large acreage that is now Lincoln High School. It
was moved to 20th in 1950.

**At 20th's dead-end, climb stairs to Market Street Drive and turn
left. Walk to 1917 and climb the stairs opposite. The thicket of
blackberries and ivy on either side is dismaying, but views are
increasingly excellent. The stairs top off at dead-end Mill Street
Terrace.** A private staircase, whose owners once graciously allowed
public access to Vista from here, is sorely missed. A garage built in
2017 occupies the stair location. A neighbor curates a poetry post,
offering a stair-climber a welcome respite.

**Walk out of the dead-end and soon you are atop the east portals
to the Vista Ridge Tunnels of US 26, also called the Sunset
Highway.** The highway was built between 1933 and 1949, and the
tunnels completed in 1970. Before the tunnels, traffic accessed the
Sunset via Jefferson Street westbound or Canyon Road eastbound.
All that rock excavated out of the mountain was dumped in the
canyon on the west side of the ridge, creating the wide roadbed we
know and love today.

Walk downhill on Mill Street Terrace. Pass Cable Avenue. From 1890 to 1904, Portland's only cable car once ran up to Portland Heights, parallel to Cable.

At 18th, go straight on the paved pedestrian path called the Ho Chi Minh Trail, adjacent to US 26.

It's noisy but brief. The name dates from the Vietnam War era, when cheap housing in Goose Hollow was home to PSU students, who made a bootleg trail along the highway between home and campus.

From the trail, turn right on 16th (the first street). Cross Montgomery and stay right, walking a steep uphill. Just south of 1815, a *cordonata* begins—a walkway with raised bars of brick or stone (in this case, concrete) designed to prevent slipping. The bars are called *cordoni*. Climb it about 25 steps then leave it via the three steps down to 16th's roadway. Walk to the dead-end. 16th's public right-of-way continues uphill under the power lines, but it's impassable now. It would make a nice pedestrian connection to Upper Hall.

At the dead-end, descend wooden stairs near an apartment building to Harrison Street. Along with 16th and College (which you'll soon be on), Harrison is one of Portland's handful of split streets, with upper and lower levels. SW Corbett and NE Wistaria are two others seen in this book.

This is a gorgeous, eclectic block. At 1501 is an 1882 Italianate home. Super grand and showy, it was owned by Morris Marks, a Polish-born shoe merchant, who built it at SW 11th and Clay. It was moved here around 1910 to make way for an apartment house. Keep this house in mind; further on is Marks' earlier home, which in 2017 was also moved. It was one of downtown's last remaining single-family homes. Next to the Marks house is a 1910 duplex and across, a 1950s ranch, all very lovely to see.

A CORDONATA

At 14th and Harrison, take a path running diagonally through a surprisingly pretty parklet owned by ODOT along I-405. The path ends at 13th and Hall. Ahead, on 13th, is a staircase. Climb to the top, College Street, and turn left.

In one block College ends at Cardinell. Turn right and climb a long staircase of false summits to upper Cardinell. Turn left. After about six homes, turn right on a gated, private road, Cardinell Way. Before you do, investigate the wooden staircase next to Cardinell Way. It drops beside a brick pump house for a 19th century Portland water system. Good photo opps. If you go down, come back up.

On Cardinell Way, walk by a clutch of 1990s homes completely suspended over airspace. At the road's U turn, go straight on a paved path across a ravine. Huge homes tower above. The path ends at Hoffman (lower road) and Sheffield (upper road). Keep left on Hoffman. Walk past one large condominium building and turn left onto a 203-step wooden staircase, called the Elevator Steps. At the bottom, turn left on Broadway Drive's sidewalk.

In the traffic island to your right is the 1880 Morris Marks house. It's not as showy as his 1882 home. The two intervening years must have been prosperous ones for the Marks family. In 2017, this house was cut in half and moved from 1134 SW 12th. The house cost the owners $1. Cutting it in half took four workers three weeks, working full time, and moving it cost $440,000. Arciform, a Portland design-build firm, is doing the restoration.

To cross the high-speed streets here, use these marked crosswalks: Follow Broadway Drive downhill to Lincoln (it comes in on the left). Turn right at the crosswalk. Now you're on Broadway, passing in front of the Marks house. Cross Grant Street. At the light, cross Broadway and 6th, then turn left to walk the sidewalk side of 6th, crossing over I-405. You're now on the campus of Portland State University. One of seven public universities in Oregon, PSU has 27,000 students. Its 50-acre campus has been evolving rapidly in the last few decades from dowdy to sparkly. For curious walkers, it's always worth investigating, to see what's new.

Look back at the hillside you just came down. The newer homes are so huge. They dwarf Piggott's Castle, once the most notable building on the hillside. It sits above the alignment of the Elevator Stairs you just came down.

In a block, turn left on Jackson, and in one more block come to Broadway. On the left is the Native American Student and Community Center. Classes in Native American studies are held here, as are public events. It's also a gathering place for the region's Native American community. To go in, check in at the reception desk. Outside, walk to "Salmon Cycle," the sculpture at the building's west end. It's by Lillian Pitt and Ken MacKintosh. Pitt, a descendant of people who have lived along the Columbia River for thousands of years, describes the sculpture:

"The pole itself... a 50 foot pole... is a log from Mt. St. Helens that we found floating in the water. It must have been there since the time of the eruption. We thought that by using it we would not be destroying any living thing, and at the same time, we would be honoring all of the creatures and plant life that once lived on that mountain.

We put giant Salmon at the top of the pole because they were, and still are, so important to the lifeways of so many Native peoples throughout the Pacific Northwest. The salmon are huge... 12 feet long... but they don't look that big because they're so high up.

And we put Salmon eggs at the bottom of the pole... and a number of other symbols going up the pole important to the Native peoples of this region."

From "Salmon Cycle," walk north on the Park Blocks, the green heart of PSU. The blocks were first planted with trees in the 1870s. Back then, homes lined them. None is left. On the left is the Viking Pavilion Regional Event Center, which opened in 2018, a reincarnation of the Peter Stott Center. On the right is Shattuck

INSIDE THE KARL MILLER CENTER AT PSU

Hall, a grade school in this once-residential neighborhood. Past it, Neuberger Hall, built in 1961 and 1969, began undergoing renovation in 2018.

After Neuberger, turn right on Harrison. In two blocks, turn left on 6th. Grab some food in the plaza and head to the fifth floor terrace at 1800 SW 6th, PSU Academic and Student Recreation Center. Adjoining the terrace is the Portland Archives. Enjoy its displays, and come back to research your house, neighborhood, or particular Portland passion. When you come back down, across the plaza is PSU's bookstore.

Catch a bus, train or streetcar here, or walk back to the start via Montgomery. It's becoming a "green street" and a bike/pedestrian route from PSU to the Willamette. As blocks and adjacent buildings get renovated, features include a curbless design and a "stormwater spine" where water runs, not in a pipe, but at the surface. In the Urban Plaza between 5th and 6th, stormwater runs in a series of stair-stepping pools. At the Karl Miller building, roof water splashes down and runs a rocky path downhill.

On the Park Blocks at Montgomery is the exuberantly detailed 1901 Simon Benson House. Moved here in 2000 from its original site at SW Park and Clay, it's now the Alumni Center. Before you reach PSU's west boundary at 12th, notice Epler Hall on the left, and its stormwater management features that make for a beautiful plaza between it and the old apartment building (now dorm) to its east.

On Montgomery, cross I-405 and 14th. Take the next right, the Ho Chi Minh Trail. It ends at 18th. Turn right. In four blocks, come to Jefferson and the MAX station where this walk began.

PSU WATER FOUNTAIN WITH WILDLIFE

Inside OHSU - VA Sky Bridge

Tilikum Crossing to Marquam Hill

S ave this 3-mile, 500-foot hill climb for a clear day when the mountains are out. The route leads over the Willamette River on beautiful Tilikum Crossing, across I-5 via the Gibbs Street pedestrian bridge, and uphill on interesting stairs, old streets and forest to Marquam Hill. There, tightly engineered slopes are home to an epic sky bridge, plus scads of stairs and four hospitals, including Oregon Health and Science University (OHSU).

There's no downhill walking: swoop back to the start via the Portland Aerial Tram. Do this on a Thursday afternoon June to October, and after you get off the tram, head to Elizabeth Caruthers Park for music and food at the South Waterfront Farmers Market. Explore the many restaurants and waterfront trail in this swath of the city, once home to heavy industry and now Portland's newest, and still-developing neighborhood.

Go to ohsu.edu, and "About OHSU" for a campus map and info about this remarkable institution. Deviate from the route, and meander its hillside—it's much friendlier to walkers than to drivers. This isn't a route to bike, especially since parts are indoors.

TILIKUM CROSSING

STAIRS, BRIDGES, AND AERIAL TRAM

- Tilikum Crossing, a pedestrian, bike and transit bridge over the Willamette River

- Darlene Hooley Pedestrian Bridge at Gibbs Street: 132 stairs (or elevator) to a bridge across I-5

- Abernethy to Barbur Blvd: 9 stairs

- Lowell between Barbur Blvd and View Point Terrace: 29 old stairs and steep sidewalk

- Terwilliger Parkway to VA Hospital: 145 stairs

- VA Hospital, "Building 16": 46 stairs

- OHSU-VA sky bridge: 660-foot, enclosed pedestrian bridge over a canyon (essentially, a tunnel in the air)

- Kohler Pavilion: 43 stairs in a rooftop sculpture garden

- Portland Aerial Tram: a 500-foot elevation drop

Start at the OMSI/SE Water Avenue MAX station at the east end of Tilikum Crossing. This bridge, opened in 2015, carries everything but cars. *Tilikum* means "people" in the Chinook trade jargon once common here—a blend of indigenous languages and English. Before dredging, the Willamette at this spot was once a shallow gravel bar, crossable on foot during the dry season—a people's crossing.

Walk west across the bridge, and find food and restrooms in OHSU's Collaborative Life Sciences Building. **From it, head south**

on **Moody,** passing under the Ross Island Bridge. This 1926 bridge got a fresh coat of paint in 2015—2018, restoring its historic deep blue-green. Pass Zidell Yards, the last manufacturer in this now completely de-industrialized waterfront. Two hundred and seventy seven barges were built here; the last was launched in June 2017. At the light near OHSU's Center for Health and Healing, **you're at the multi-tasking Gibbs/Moody intersection**. Watch for bikes, runners, a streetcar, automobiles, and overhead, an aerial tram.

Climb the five-story staircase to the Gibbs Street bridge. It was dedicated in 2012 to honor Darlene Hooley, who served 12 years in the US Congress. **Once across, walk straight one block on Gibbs, then left on Corbett.** This is old South Portland (aka Lair Hill in this area). In the 1870s, the city's first streetcar, horse-drawn, ran down 1st a few blocks west, crossing under the path of today's aerial tram. What a difference 130 years can make. **Five blocks later, turn**

OHSU to VA Hospital sky bridge

right on Lane Street. A Portland Heritage Tree, an Oregon white oak, is on the corner.

Walk a block to Water and turn left. In one block, come to Abernethy; on the right, climb nine stairs to Barbur and turn right. At a painted crosswalk, carefully cross two lanes of a Ross Island Bridge on-ramp. Once across, walk right on a grassy pedestrian peninsula to a painted crosswalk. Carefully (sight lines are good) cross two lanes of Barbur to an island. Cross two more and turn left on Barbur's sidewalk. Cross Lane; at View Point Terrace, stay left and low on Barbur's sidewalk. It curves right, around an underpass. Soon after that, climb the Lowell staircase. It tops off at a sidewalk so steep it should have a rope tow. Keep climbing to View Point Terrace. A fantastic Queen Anne Victorian gives you something to look at while you take a few breaths. Keep climbing the rope-tow sidewalk.

At the top is your reward, **beautiful Condor Avenue. Turn right,** and enjoy its blend of home ages and styles. If the gates are open at 3990, look through to Mt. Hood. Further, views of downtown through giant bamboo are fantastic. **At Condor Lane, the first left, turn left and walk uphill** on the right shoulder to avoid a blind curve. A massive California redwood grows on the right.

Cross Terwilliger and climb an elegant staircase to the VA Hospital. This is one of the city's loveliest staircases. Portland Parks owns the land along its lower half. Uncle Sam owns the top part. The staircase designer had a thing for eights: 13 flights of eight stairs, plus five more flights, for a total 145 stairs.

At the top is a lovely building with a dull name: Building 16. **Go left and climb 46 stairs on its south side. Ahead is the 1980s-blue Portland VA Medical Center. Follow the sidewalk to the right,** following "Main Entrance" signs; don't wander left into the parking garage (as I did), where the smell of last-ditch cigarettes

Forest steps, Terwilliger Parkway to VA Hospital

will choke you. Instead, stay on the sidewalk that curls uphill. Follow the blue wall. It leads to the main entrance.

Inside, you're on the first floor. Take the elevator to the second floor. From the elevator hall, turn left then quick left. Ahead a sign says "Sky Bridge to OHSU." Walk the bridge and enjoy the spectacular views and the whole amazing vibe in this air tunnel. I like to sit and listen to conversational snippets that flow by. The sky bridge opened in 1992. Doernbecher Children's Hospital is west of the sky bridge.

At the other end of the bridge, you're in OHSU Hospital, at a coffee shop. OHSU is Oregon's only academic health center, as well as a research university. On this relatively small space on Marquam Hill it has 36 major buildings. A grocery here is a good place to buy a snack that you can eat outdoors at the Kohler Pavilion.

Just past the gift shop, follow signs to the Peter Kohler Pavilion or the Portland Aerial Tram. Downhill rides are free. Before you board the tram, head to the Pavilion's sky-high, sculpture-filled terraces for wondrous views of the city and Cascade peaks. On the lower pavilion, more stairs lead down and across to Marquam Hill's fourth hospital, Shriners, with its logo of a fez-wearing Shriner holding a child. It serves children free of charge.

Ride the tram over old South Portland, and cross the Tilikum Crossing Bridge over the Willamette to return to the start.

Part of the Iowa Street steps from Johns Landing, under Barbur Blvd, and up into George Himes Park

Terwilliger Parkway to Willamette River

This 4-mile route is bookended by two long and quite different staircases. It starts on historic Terwilliger Parkway, on the east flank of the Tualatin Mountains, passes through the lush Fulton Community Garden, crosses I-5 at a rare residential crossing into the big-view Fulton neighborhood, and descends to a beach at Willamette Park.

Do it on a late summer day when the garden is at peak beauty, and river levels are low enough to walk beaches or swim a bit. If you want to wade or beach-walk, bring water-worthy shoes, as the silty/sandy shore may be rocky or a bit mucky. Food options are about two-thirds of the way through the loop, which loses about 525 feet and gains about 625 feet.

An optional 0.8-mile loop to a long, obscure staircase explores one of those hard-to-access, but in-plain-sight neighborhoods that occupy West Hills niches.

STAIRS AND PATHS

- 5th to Capitol Highway: 36 stairs

- Custer steps, Kelly to Taylors Ferry: 100 stairs

- Willamette Park stairs to river: 13 stairs

- Iowa stairs under I-5 and Barbur Boulevard in George Himes Park: 186 stairs

- Parkhill Steps (on optional loop): 147 stairs

- Beach walking (during low water levels): Willamette Moorage Park to Willamette Park

PUBLIC GREENSPACE ACROSS FROM 7535 SW MILES PLACE

Start at SW Nebraska Street and Terwilliger Parkway. TriMet's buses 39 and 65 stop here; parking on Nebraska is limited to two hours.

Walk south on Terwilliger Parkway, the only scenic parkway the city constructed after the famous Olmsted Brothers landscape design firm recommended a citywide system of parkways and parks in 1903.

After crossing Chestnut, turn left at 7040 onto a footpath through what looks like private property. This is the Nevada Street right-of-way. At the end, turn right on curbless, country-feeling 5th; at its end, descend stairs to Barbur. Walk left on its sidewalk to cross at a light at 3rd and enter the voluptuous Fulton Community Garden. In the garden, at 7420, pass a home from this area's bucolic 1890s. **Turn left at a junction and follow the gravel road.** Ahead is the Fulton Park Community Center, built in 1914 as a school, and now leased by Portland Parks & Recreation. It's at Miles and Brier Place. If you like scenic blocks, turn left at Brier Place for an out-and-back look at a pretty residential street that ends at Barbur.

From the community center, turn right on Brier Place and cross over I-5. Immediately past I-5, on your right is Custer Street. Super intriguing; you may want to investigate. Brier Place curves and becomes Custer, a street of expanding views the further east you walk.

On Custer, walk three blocks to Kelly, to the start of 100 stairs. Descend. Flights are interrupted by three streets, all eminently worth exploring, and long, steep sidewalks that must be some of the city's most exciting sled runs.

At the bottom of the stairs, turn left on the sidewalk along Taylors Ferry Road. Past Virginia, cross to the sidewalk in a landscaped island, then cross Macadam at the light, and keep straight on Miles Street.

Cross over the Willamette Shore Line tracks. It provided passenger service between Portland and Oswego (now Lake Oswego) from 1887 to 1929. After that, it was freight only. In 1988, a century after passengers first rode its rails, a consortium of jurisdictions and agencies bought the right-of-way to revive it as a streetcar line. Members are Metro, Lake Oswego, Portland, Clackamas and Multnomah counties, Oregon Department of Transportation, and TriMet. TriMet holds the title. The Willamette Shore Trolley runs excursion trains in the summer, but residents along the route resisted a commuter line, and the idea was shelved in 2012.

Before walking out onto Miles Place, watch for fast-moving cyclists. This charming little block of houseboats-turned-permanent homes is part of the Willamette Greenway Trail. If you turn right, at the end of Miles Place (across from 7535) is an unmarked greenspace; it's the north end of 16-acre Willamette Moorage Park. You can walk through and out to the river. The riverfront slice of land to the north (behind the homes) is public, so at low water you can walk from here into Willamette Park, where a short stone staircase will lead to park paths.

The land and riverfront south of Miles Place's dead-end is also Willamette Moorage Park. Weber Brothers Tannery operated here from 1894 to the 1940s. A 1900 Oregonian ad noted that oak bark was brought in from Humboldt County, California to tan harness leather and other products. Goods were shipped out via the rail line you just crossed over. Stephens Creek flows into the Willamette here; restoration work completed in 2008 improved side-channel habitat for salmon, trout and lamprey. The floating home moorage here has been owned by the City since 1953 when it purchased the tannery property.

If you stay on Miles Place rather than walking the beach: at its north end, enter 27-acre Willamette Park. In 2017, many improvements were completed. Walk the riverfront trail; in a bit, descend 12 stone steps to the water if you haven't already been down to the river. Notice the rocky islet just offshore.

In June 1953 the Oregonian noted that the land here "flooded almost every year." The flooding was great for wildlife, providing off-channel habitat for fish, but it ended in 1969 when debris from the demolition of the Oregon Journal building was placed here.

Inland, walk across the park to the brown concrete building, the Hannah Mason Pump Station. Completed in 2017, it was inspired in part by that rocky islet. The exterior is designed, like the islet, to interact with its environment. Lichen and mosses will find good purchase on its rough concrete, and water spilling over the rooftop garden will add streaks of mineralization. Over time, it will blend more into the landscape. Pumps inside lift Bull Run water to customers in the West Hills. Most Bull Run water flows solely by gravity from the Bull Run watershed to end users, but West Hills water users require pump stations like this one to lift the water to them. This replaced a 1912 pump station, and uses much less electricity, not only because pumps are more energy efficient but because it pulls water from a supply line at a significantly higher hydraulic elevation.

Hannah Mason once owned the land where the station sits. A resident of Northwest Portland and widow of Portland mayor William S. Mason, she died in 1908. He was president of a bank during the Financial Panic of 1893. In the era before the Federal Deposit Insurance Corporation protected depositors from bank failures, bank customers would lose everything they had on deposit when a bank became illiquid. Rather than let depositors lose their funds, she turned over $113,000 of her own money to her husband to pay them. Hard to imagine a CEO (or their spouse) of any modern bank taking care of us little guys like that.

Explore more of the park: the boat dock, the floating sidewalk adjacent it, the natural habitat/shoreline north of the dock, and the deluxe off leash dog park.

Opposite of the dog park, leave the park via Nebraska. Cross Macadam at the light and find good eating options on this corner.

On Nebraska two blocks west of Macadam, turn right onto Corbett. To the left, Corbett splits into upper and lower levels, which may or may not be of interest. To the right is a cute 1929 garden apartment complex. North of it, a lineup of 1920s homes sits opposite a Portland public school built in 1928. Still owned by PPS, it's leased to a private school now. Pass another Water Bureau pump station.

Turn left on Iowa. Where it ends, walk into a driveway, following the SW Trails sign pointing to a stair path. Here begins a climb up many flights of stairs interrupted by stretches of trail. Pass under I-5 and then under Barbur's wooden trestle, (they use wood to hold up this road?) Side paths that are service roads offer unique perspectives.

Keep on the main trail up an ivy-choked creek valley. Not super scenic, but interesting. Cross over the creek, climb the last 28 stairs and where the trail Ts, turn right. Follow it out to Terwilliger Parkway and turn left. In 0.2 mile, you're back at the start.

Parkhill Optional Loop: 0.8 mile. From Terwilliger and Nebraska, walk east on Nebraska. Big views! Take a sharp right on Parkhill Drive and walk downhill to Barbur. Turn left, facing traffic in the bike lane, walking 200 feet to the base of a staircase. Climb its 147 steps. At the top, turn left on Parkhill Drive and right on Nebraska to return to the start.

A VERY OLD STAIRCASE IN THE ORIGINAL
40 ACRES OF WASHINGTON PARK, AND ITS
NEW, INCOMPLETE SIGNPOST.

Washington Park, Arlington Heights, and Rose Garden

This 4.5-mile, 800+ stair walk explores land owned by Amos Nahum King (1822 to 1901), once so poor he went shoeless from March to December. By the end of his life, he was a wealthy landowner, living on the hill that bears his name. This route covers some of King's large holdings, primarily in Washington Park.

Grab a pre-walk coffee at the site of a brickworks owned by Amos's son-in-law, and spend an hour or so on the route on a side trip, either at the park's famous Portland Japanese Garden or International Rose Test Garden. Roses bloom from May through November, with the peak, of course, during Rose Festival month, June. They are most beautiful with grey, moody sky as backdrop. Service animals only in the Japanese Garden. At walk's end, find just the meal you're looking for on NW 23rd Avenue.

STAIRS

- Burnside at 24th Place to the *Coming of the White Man*: 280 stairs

- Marconi stair path to Peanut Bowl and Parkside Drive: 52 stairs

- Parkside Lane to Tichner Drive: 23 stairs

- Champlain to Fairview Blvd: 83 stairs

- Fairview to Kingston above Japanese Garden: 82 stairs

- Kingston to Rose Garden Promenade: 49 stairs

- Rose Garden Amphitheater: 38 stairs

- Promenade to Rose Garden Way: 27 stairs

- Lewis and Clark Drive to Osage Street: 175 stairs

Start at the MAX Providence Park station, SW 18th and Morrison. Walk to 20th and Morrison. The US Bank here is where Amos and Melinda King built a house in 1856, three years before Oregon became a state. The home stood along the Tuality Road, a wagon route hewn into wilderness in 1845 by Francis Pettygrove. It ran from the tiny Portland townsite over the mountains and into the Tualatin Valley. It's now called Burnside Street.

The Kings owned a tannery they could look down on from their home. In vats holding hemlock bark and water, cow hides soaked for months, softening into wearable leather for clothing, saddles, and harnesses. The tannery was in a hollow along the banks of Tanner Creek, where Providence Park now stands. By the time the neighborhood began evolving from wilderness to poshness in the 1870s, the tannery was gone. Amos, an avid gardener, walked the streets around here in his old age, picking up trash and showing off his prize potatoes.

When it opened as Multnomah Stadium in 1926, Providence Park was owned by the Multnomah Amateur Athletic Club, or MAAC, which is still adjacent to its south end. The MAC (having dropped the "Amateur" in the 1930s) sold the stadium to the City of Portland in the 1960s.

At 20th, turn right and cross Burnside for snacks or coffee in the Fred Meyer Stadium store. It sits atop E.J. Jeffery's brickyard. The third floor balcony offers fantastic views of the area you're about to explore.

On Burnside, walk uphill past interesting old apartment buildings and sundry cafes and shops to 24th Place, the original Washington Park entrance, until 1903. It's on the South (left) side of Burnside. This deeply forested hillside is part of the park's first 40 acres, which Amos King sold to the City in 1871.

At the park entrance, take the stairs on the right, the start of a 280-step stair path. As you climb, Portland Parks' work to remove ivy and replant with rhododendrons and other native blooming shrubs is yielding beautiful results. A century-old tree blocks the path, and a succession of gardeners have left it alone. The stair path crosses a loop road and tops off at a sculpture, "The Coming of the White Man," two Native Americans looking worriedly and excitedly at Lewis and Clark's approach on the Columbia River.

Walk west, leaving the park. Turn left at the first residential street on its boundary, Wright.

Wright used to border on the elk enclosure when this area housed Portland's first zoo. As the neighborhood developed, homeowners objected to the animals, so they were moved to the area downhill of what later became the rose garden. On the left is a Tudor restroom building and the park's Oregon Holocaust Memorial; its interpretive displays and cast bronze objects are deeply moving and disturbing. Spend time in contemplation there now or on another visit.

From Wright, turn right on residential Park Place (not the park entrance road). At Marconi, re-enter the park by climbing the basalt stair-path to a hidden field, the Peanut Bowl. At its far side follow the footpath; at a sharp right, keep on the path (not the roadway) as it climbs a slope and stairs. There used to be a house here; it slid off the slope in the 1930s.

The stair path ends at Parkside Drive. Turn right. Look up, left, at one of the city's grandest homes, the A.H. Maegly house, completed in 1915. It was designed by John Bennes, prolific architect of the Hollywood Theatre among other commissions. His Chicago roots are evident in the home's Prairie-meets-Italian villa style.

Turn right on Parkside Lane, an easily overlooked, single-lane gem with beautiful landscaping. It ends in a staircase. Descend to Tichner and turn left, and left on Kingston. Grand homes abound, including the front of the Maegly house.

Turn right on Fairview and right on lovely Rutland Terrace. Take it slow to enjoy its intriguing homes and landscapes. Turn left on Champlain. At 2864, climb stairs. This is Portland's only public staircase to split a property owner's yard.

At the top, turn left onto Fairview Blvd. Across from 2911 once sat the Canterbury Castle (see photos online), one man's folly. Besieged by troubles ranging from geologic to structural to fiscal, it was demolished in 2009. A visible remnant of its stone garage hints at the story.

Where Fairview hairpins downhill pass Cascade Drive, look right for a trail into Washington Park (across from Champlain Drive). Take the trail; at a fork keep left and soon you're walking above homes on Fairview, with great views of the neighborhood. On the right is the Portland Japanese Garden. Stairs on this trail total 82.

At the bottom, Kingston, pay the fee and enjoy the Japanese Garden, or come back another time. Ahead and on the left is Washington Park's free International Rose Test Garden. Descend stairs between the tennis courts and then down to the main promenade. Plenty of stairs and meanders here to enjoy, at Portland's number one tourist attraction, with 500,000 visitors each year.

From Memorial Day to Labor Day, take the free daily garden tour at 1 p.m. Tours start outside the gift shop, and are led by an OSU Master Gardener, one of the 400 Friends of the International Rose Test Garden. Other volunteers staff the Master Gardener booth; still others, wonderfully named "deadheaders," do double duty: while pruning spent blooms, they're de facto Portland ambassadors, answering questions about roses, the city, the park, and "What's the name of that mountain?"

SOME OF THE MANY ROSE GARDEN STAIRS AND THEIR TOURISTS.

Restrooms and the gift shop are at the south end of promenade. In 2016 the promenade received a facelift, making it accessible to all by removing stairs, adding ramps and rails, and replacing a bumpy walkway.

Near the garden's north end, you may want to hang out in the amphitheater on the right. Its stage and grassy steps are a great place to picnic.

Exit the garden via steps at the promenade's north end and turn right on Rose Garden Way. Pass Reservoir 3 on the right. At 2018 this open-air reservoir was midway through its rebuilding. It is being converted to a closed, belowground and seismically reinforced reservoir, with a reflecting pool atop it. Design began on this massive project in 2012. In 2020, construction will stop for two years to let soils settle. (It and Reservoir 4, downhill, were built in the 1890s within the body of a landslide, reactivating it; the hill has been moving ever since.) When construction resumes, the reflecting pool, which will adhere to the old reservoir's footprint, will be installed, along with a grand staircase leading to a pathway around the pool's perimeter. Reservoir 4 stays online until 2020, when it is converted to wildlife habitat and a bioswale.

Beyond the reservoir, at the old fountain, keep left, walking against car traffic on Lewis & Clark Circle. The sculpture of Sacajawea with her baby Pomp is on your right. Beyond it, near the park's east boundary, begin the descent on several long flights of stairs. They'll take you down to Burnside, where restaurants are awaiting your business along NW 23rd Avenue.

STAIRS IN THE CUPOLA OF THE PIONEER COURTHOUSE

Downtown and the Pearl District

Explore the civic buildings that belong to you, Citizen, as well as a couple of privately owned public spaces. This 2.5-mile one-way walk with a MAX return, or 5-mile walking loop, explores spaces that each merit side-wandering and discovering. The route visits three federal courthouses, among many other fascinating places. Ride MAX back to the start, or walk back via the riverfront.

Pioneer Courthouse, the Mark O. Hatfield US Courthouse, and City Hall are open weekdays during business hours. The courthouses require a pass through security with government photo ID. Children do not need photo ID. City Hall has a security check too. The Armory's lobby opens at 10 a.m. weekdays and noon on weekends.

LILLEY GRAND STAIRCASE

PORTLAND ARMORY STAIRCASE

STAIRS

- Portland State University's Urban Center and Karl Miller Center: various stairs inside and out

- City Hall: 77 stairs to the fourth floor

- Gus J. Solomon U.S. Courthouse: 25 stairs to entrance

- Central Library: 76 stairs to the third floor

- Pioneer Courthouse Square: around 25 outdoor stairs

- Pioneer Courthouse: 115 stairs to the fifth floor cupola

- Powell's City of Books: 58 stairs to the top floor Pearl Room

- Armory: 25 stairs to a second-floor balcony

- Natural Capital Center: 75 stairs in the outdoor stair tower to third floor terrace

- Union Station: 51 indoor stairs to the third floor, and 86 stairs bracketing a pedestrian bridge over the rail yard.

OUTSIDE STAIRS AT THE NATURAL CAPITAL CENTER LEAD TO THIS ROOFTOP TERRACE

Begin at PSU Urban Center, the block bounded by 5th, 6th, Montgomery, and Mill. This is one of Portland's busiest transit hubs. A streetcar runs through it, and MAX trains stop at it, as do numerous buses. PSU's bookstore is here, along with its Academic and Student Recreation Center and various restaurants. The beautiful Karl Miller Center (the School of Business) to the west opened in 2017 and stands in stark contrast to the Brutalism of the "old PSU" parking garage next door. The campus in recent decades has transformed itself from a half-acknowledged stepchild of downtown to one of its most beautiful areas for a walker to explore. Cross 6th to explore the open atrium in the Karl Miller Center, with its stairs for studying, eating, visiting, and climbing. The exterior wood is Alaska yellow cedar.

From the center, walk north on 6th. Don't miss one of the city's best green walls, at the Hotel Modera, north of Clay on 6th. After Columbia, on your left is the former *Oregonian* building, where stories were written and papers printed. It's a 1948 design by Pietro Belluschi. Now it's creative office space.

Cross Jefferson and turn right; after 5th, you're walking alongside City Hall, your next stop. Turn left to enter it on 4th. City Hall was constructed in 1895 and renovated in 1998. Besides bringing the building up to seismic and other building codes, the renovation restored original features, such as two light wells that bring daylight into interior spaces. In the 1930s, they had been closed to create storage and office space. Go climb one of the two interior staircases that flank the two light wells. Their filigreed plated cast-iron balustrades, cast bronze stair risers and marble treads are original. Climb to the fourth floor, for a total of 77 stairs. The nearby elevators were added in 1910.

See the columns around the stairs? They look like stone, but they're plaster decorated in a technique called scagliola. In it, pigmented plaster is the base; veining is created by drawing strands of raw silk saturated in other pigments through the wet plaster; other layers of pigment can be troweled on and then cut back to resemble natural color variation in stone. When dry, the surface is pumiced smooth, then buffed with oiled felt. Beeswax is sometimes used as a finishing agent.

From City Hall, turn left on Madison. Stop at 5th to appreciate Portlandia, our city's beloved sculpture perched, to your right, at the Portland Building, which, no surprise, was designed in the 1980s. Continue on Madison. After you cross 6th, look right to the back of the Gus J. Solomon US Courthouse. When it was built in 1933, covering an entire city block, the future looked dim for the quaint 1875 Pioneer Courthouse, seen later in the route; its demolition was considered. Ironically the Pioneer Courthouse is now a working courthouse and this, its replacement, is not. The US District Court left this building in 1997 and moved to the new Mark O. Hatfield US Courthouse; that courthouse is seen near the end of the route. At the Gus Solomon Courthouse building, interior spaces are now occupied by various government agencies, lawyers, and the Classroom Law Project, which teaches Portland teenagers Constitutional law. If you have time, go in to look around the gorgeous Art Deco lobby, formerly a post office.

Still on Madison, cross Broadway, then pass through the linear forest that is the South Park Blocks and to the Portland Art Museum and its controversial Madison Street pedestrian corridor. Plans are for the large open space between the two major museum buildings to become a new entrance, the Rothko Pavilion. Pedestrian advocacy during its design resulted in retaining a part of the historic, open passageway. It's named for Mark Rothko, who moved to Portland in 1913 as a 10 year old.

If the pedestrian walkway is under construction, walk around it and rejoin the route at 10th and Madison.

At the end of the walkway, at 10th and Madison, turn right on 10th. Here is Portland's first Heritage Tree, planted in someone's front yard. It's an American elm. In 1958 a YWCA was built at the site.

Stay on 10th three blocks and come to Central Library, at 821 SW 10th. This 1913 library is the flagship of the 19 libraries and one bookstore operated by Multnomah County. A 1997 renovation stripped away midcentury vinyl floors, drop ceilings, and fluorescent lights. As you enter, a black granite staircase pulls you in for a closer look. Its treads and risers are incised with garden-themed art. A library, as everyone knows, is a garden of knowledge. The stairs replaced the original marble stairs, which had worn down. The marble stairs still exist between the second and third floors.

Look for the garden motif elsewhere in the building. Don't miss "Preserving a Memory," a much-caressed bronze tree in the Children's Library; its bark combines elements of Oregon's natural history with subjects found in the Dewey Decimal System.

From the library, walk east on Yamhill three blocks. At Broadway is Pioneer Courthouse Square. Explore its stairs, art, and interior spaces, where Travel Portland volunteers answer questions. Sit on the steps watching the human parade. Experience the all gender restroom, the city's busiest, installed in 2017. Three hundred thousand people use the square's toilets each year.

The square itself is also a hard-working piece of real estate. It hosts 300 events and welcomes 10 million visitors each year. A nonprofit, Pioneer Courthouse Square, manages its docket of events. After all this use, Portland's "living room" as the square is called, needed some repairs. In 2017, a major renovation fixed the membrane below the bricks that was allowing water into interior spaces below.

From the square, cross 6th and enter the Pioneer Courthouse. Completed in 1875, it is one of four primary locations where the United States Court of Appeals for the Ninth Circuit hears oral arguments. It also houses the chambers (offices) of Portland-based judges of the Ninth Circuit. In 1869, as a federal courthouse, post office and customs house, it was criticized for its remoteness from the city.

In 2005, a seismic renovation was completed. The entire building now sits on 75 friction pendulum base isolators that will allow up to 18 inches of movement during an earthquake.

Many Portlanders don't know they can go inside and explore this treasure. The American traditions it represents inspire pride, and its interpretive displays are informative. An hour here feels a bit like a visit to Washington, D.C. Between the first and fourth floors, climb wooden staircases with ornate wooden balustrades. Inside are meeting rooms, attorney rooms, libraries, and the former lobby for the post office, which occupied the first floor until 2003. Period wool carpets cover the floors. Most wondrous is a nineteenth-century,

A WORKING COURTROOM IN THE PIONEER COURTHOUSE

paneled courtroom on the second floor, with one of the building's six fireplaces. It is an active courtroom, so it may not be accessible at all times. You can enter any room with an open door. Come in to watch oral arguments before the justices, scheduled mornings at various times throughout the year.

Most fun for stair-lovers are steps to the glassed-in, eight-sided cupola, a one-room fifth floor accessible only by stair. It's an urban tree house, with 360-degree views of downtown. A stair ladder leads to the roof for flag-changing. That one's off limits.

From the Courthouse, walk west (uphill) on Morrison and turn right on 11th. In this block is the Sentinel Hotel, a former Elks Temple. It was built in 1923 modeled after the Farnese Palace in Rome. It's a wondrous example of Italian Renaissance architecture. Go in and look at the ceiling in the lobby. Wowsa. The Elks lost the building during the Depression.

Keep on 11th, and cross Burnside. From here north, streets are alphabetical, which helps when orienting oneself. At Couch, go into Powell's City of Books, in a former car dealership. Climb a staircase and see which room it deposits you at. Gold, purple, red, green…each room has its genres, and breed of browsers. It's easy to lose a few hours of your life at Powell's.

When you emerge from Powell's, keep north on 11th one block. Here is Portland Center Stage at the Armory (128 NW 11th). When it was erected in 1891, the Armory was surrounded by homes, churches, and schools. Soldiers mustered here in 1898 for the Spanish American War; eventually its medieval stylings were anachronistic and unneeded. It languished for decades as an ersatz event space until 1968, when Blitz Weinhard, which brewed beer on Burnside, started storing kegs here.

In 2006, the renovated building, with its dull white paint job removed, became home to Portland Center Stage. Everything in this building is new. Originally, there was nothing under the wooden roof trusses but open space. Bring in a coffee or scone, climb the beautiful stairs and find a seat by a narrow gun port window. It's a lovely space to take a break from the streets.

From the Armory, turn right on Davis and left on 10th. Just past Irving, on the right, is the Natural Capital Center. Enter it on 10th. This 1895 warehouse is owned by Ecotrust Properties and houses businesses and organizations that combine profitability with stewardship and environmental sustainability. Get food in the lobby then go outside and climb the 75 stairs in the outdoor stair tower to the third floor terrace. The two stair towers act as seismic reinforcement to this unreinforced masonry building.

Walk north on 10th, passing Jamison Square. Its stone stairs become fountains in warm weather.

Along its north end, pass through a lush linear park between two buildings. At the end, Lovejoy, turn right, then left on 9th. Next to Station Place Tower, take the lower sidewalk alongside Lovejoy Street's sidewalk, which rises to the right. The sidewalk ends at Station Way. Ahead is a nice view of the Broadway Bridge, and to the left, the Fremont Bridge. **Turn right on Station Way, walking under Lovejoy, then under Broadway, both of which rise here to join at the Broadway Bridge.**

Walk to the front of Union Station (800 NW 6th) and go in. Built in 1896, it's now owned by the City of Portland. Its Italian Renaissance design has friendly, striped window awnings, and decorative iron scrollwork. I like the winged train wheels, outside above the second story windows. The neon "Go by Train" sign on the tower dates from 1948.

Inside travertine and marble floors are wax-shiny, and marble walls reflect neon signs to "Baggage Dept," "Newsstand," and "Telephones." Have a small business? You can rent space upstairs. Follow the restrooms sign and then the sign to "South Stairway." Climb the old staircase. Wood flooring, transom windows, original doors, lights, wainscoting, exit signs, and that indefinable old building smell take you back a century or so. Come back outside or hang out at Wilf's, an old fashioned bar and steakhouse in the station.

To end the walk, ride MAX back to the start. The station is at NW 5th and Glisan.

To walk back along the riverfront, cross the train tracks via the pedestrian bridge; it leads to Station Place Apartments. Cross through them and cross Naito Parkway at a crosswalk. Keep straight and end up on the greenway path along the Willamette.

Turn right on the path (actually a paved sidewalk), and cross under the Steel Bridge. Here begins Tom McCall Waterfront Park. Walk the park, passing under the Burnside and Morrison bridges, to Salmon Street Springs. It's turned off in winter—look for it where you see a bowl-like staircase just north of the Hawthorne Bridge.

Leave the park and head to 3rd and Salmon to visit the city's newest federal courthouse, the Mark O. Hatfield United States Courthouse, 1000 SW 3rd. Check out its 8th floor sculpture garden.

Afterwards, head back to the start.

AT PIONEER COURTHOUSE SQUARE

Willamette River Bridges, Stairs, and Paths

I n Portland, 12 bridges cross the Willamette River. Nine allow pedestrians and cyclists, and six of those do a great job of it, with wide sidewalks and easy street connections, Those six bridges are Sellwood, Tilikum Crossing, Hawthorne, Morrison (south side), Steel, and Broadway. Burnside's pretty good. St. Johns has sidewalks but they're narrow and close to the fast traffic. Still worth it. Ross Island: I'd skip.

Five of the Willamette's downtown bridges have staircases connecting them to streets under them or to ramps. Some of these staircases are in the route on page 177. Other staircases, which are described in the following pages, are useful if you happen to need them, but don't work up into especially enjoyable walking routes. One big change from my first stairs book: many downtown staircases and the under-bridge areas around them have become permanent refuges for homeless folk.

On the west side, Willamette bridges are connected by riverfront trails (with some inland sections). From the Sellwood Bridge, the Willamette Greenway Trail runs north through Governor Tom McCall Waterfront Park, ending at the Steel Bridge. The trail continues in various guises as a greenway path across private properties to beyond the Fremont Bridge.

On the east side, from the Sellwood Bridge, the Springwater Trail runs north to the Central Eastside Industrial District. From there, near Tilikum Crossing, the Vera Katz Eastbank Esplanade runs north to the Steel Bridge. From it you can bike city streets about 0.3 miles to the last walkable downtown bridge, the Broadway.

Bridges are listed in the order encountered if you were drifting in an inner tube (which you might want to do).

Sellwood Bridge

The Sellwood Bridge opened in 2016, entirely replacing a 1925 bridge that has since been torn down. It needs no stairs to connect its wide pedestrian/bike sidewalk to east- and west-side streets and paths.

SELLWOOD BRIDGE

Ross Island Bridge

This 1926 bridge has no stairs. It does have a narrow sidewalk on its north side, but traffic is fast and close, and the exit off the bridge does not have walkers in mind. Not recommended.

Tilikum Crossing

This 2015 bridge is for walkers, bikers, and mass transit. It needs no stairs; smooth transitions lead to paths to other walkable bridges. It's a beauty, instantly beloved by Portlanders from the day it first started emerging above the water.

TILIKUM CROSSING

Marquam Bridge

This Interstate Highway bridge (I-405) has no stairs and no pedestrian access.

Hawthorne Bridge

This 1910 vertical lift bridge is so photogenic, with its red-orange counterweights and green paint job. Add a blue sky with puffy clouds and what could be better? Very busy with cyclists and bikers. Crossing it is a quintessential Portland experience.

HAWTHORNE BRIDGE

Westside stairs

- 36, from Waterfront Park to westbound bridge sidewalk

- 37, from Waterfront Park to eastbound bridge sidewalk

- 23, from southbound Naito Parkway to westbound bridge ramp leading to 1st and Main

Eastside stairs

- ▪▪▪ 7, from Madison west of Water to ramp leading to westbound bridge sidewalk

- ▪▪▪ 45, from Madison and Water to westbound bridge approach

- ▪▪▪ 50, from Hawthorne at 1st to eastbound bridge ramp and bus stop

- ▪▪▪ 45, from Hawthorne at 3rd to southbound ramp heading toward MLK, Jr. Blvd

Morrison Bridge

Opened in 1958, this bridge has a bike-friendly upgrade: a wide and separated-from-traffic sidewalk on its eastbound side. Take it to the beautiful spiral ramp that leads down to the Eastbank Esplanade.

Westside stairs

- ▪▪▪ 23, from north of Morrison between Naito and 1st to eastbound bridge sidewalk

- ▪▪▪ 14, from 1st to Alder, east of 2nd

- ▪▪▪ 14, from 1st to Washington

- ▪▪▪ 25, between Naito and 1st, south of Stark, to bridge ramp leading to southbound Naito

Eastside stairs

- ▪▪▪ 49, from west of Water and Morrison to westbound bridge approach lanes (east of I-5)

- ▪▪▪ 30 down, 25 up, hanging from westbound bridge ramp over Esplanade

- 29 down, 25 up, hanging from bridge deck east of Water near Morrison to westbound bridge sidewalk

- 42, from south of Water and Belmont to eastbound bridge ramp

- Spiral ramp from Esplanade to eastbound bridge sidewalk

Burnside Bridge

This 1926 bridge has its charms, pretty good sidewalks, and interesting staircases.

BURNSIDE BRIDGE

Westside stairs

- 30, from 1st to eastbound bridge sidewalk

- 31, from 1st to westbound bridge sidewalk

Eastside stairs

■▪■ 86, from Esplanade to eastbound bridge sidewalk

Steel Bridge

This multi-tasking, double-deck bridge from 1912 carries freight and passenger trains, MAX light rail trains, cars, buses, cyclists, and walkers on its two decks. The Eastbank Esplanade/Waterfront Park loop between the Hawthorne and Steel bridges feeds walkers and cyclists onto the Steel's lower deck. The sidewalk there can get pretty congested, and if the lower deck gets lifted, you've reached a temporary dead-end. The upper deck sidewalks are less used.

STEEL BRIDGE

Westside stairs

■▪■ 57, from Waterfront Park to eastbound upper deck bridge sidewalk

Eastside stairs

- 65, from Esplanade to eastbound upper deck bridge sidewalk

Broadway Bridge

This 1913 bridge is super charming, maybe not as pretty as the St. Johns or Hawthorne, but close. It has wide sidewalks on both sides, and its staircases have the most panache of any bridge in town.

BROADWAY BRIDGE

Westside stairs

- 81, from southbound Naito to eastbound bridge sidewalk (pictured)

- 82, from southbound Naito to westbound bridge sidewalk

- 20, from Irving at Union Station parking lot to northbound bridge sidewalk

- 26, from lower level of Broadway, north of Hoyt, to southbound Broadway sidewalk

Eastside stairs

- 27, from southbound Interstate to eastbound bridge sidewalk

Fremont Bridge

Like the Marquam Bridge, which is its partner in the I-405 loop, the Fremont has no stairs and no pedestrian access.

FREMONT BRIDGE

Burlington Northern Railroad Bridge 5.1

This gorgeous bridge can be experienced only from an Amtrak train. It's owned by BNSF Railway, which allows no access. The 5.1 refers to the distance in miles to Union Station.

RAILROAD BRIDGE

St. Johns Bridge

See p.17 for a stair walk that puts you on the two staircases related (but not connected) to this bridge, by far most everyone's favorite. Does a day exist when it doesn't appear in someone's social media feed?

St. John's Bridge with Greenpeace protestors

PORTLAND MAYOR VERA KATZ

Columbia River Bridges, Stairs, and Paths

PORTLAND HAS FOUR COLUMBIA RIVER BRIDGES. ALTHOUGH the first two are part of the Interstate Highway system, they accommodate walkers and bikers. Views from the Interstate Bridge, despite the noise and traffic, are superb. The four bridges are listed from upstream to downstream.

Glenn Jackson Bridge (I-205)

The I-205 Bike Path runs down the middle, squeezed between eight lanes of high-speed traffic. Not scenic. On foot, it's too loud, too long, and too exposed to be enjoyable. On a bike it's bearable, but not too fun. No stairs.

Interstate Bridge (I-5)

Both north- and southbound lanes have a sidewalk on their outside edges, resulting in great views for walkers of the Columbia River, boat slips, houseboat moorages, and Mt. Hood. Access is tricky. Download the "I-5 Bridge Map" from the City of Vancouver so you don't get annoyed with the labyrinthine approaches.

Oregon Slough Railroad Bridge (Bridge 8.8) and Burlington Northern Railroad Bridge 9.6

These bridges were built in 1908 and are owned by BNSF Railway. Amtrak is the only way to experience them. The Oregon Slough Bridge runs between Marine Drive to Hayden Island. Bridge 9.6 runs between Hayden Island and Vancouver, Washington. No pedestrian access is allowed. Train traffic is frequent. The numbers refer to the distance in miles to Union Station.

Joining the Citizen Stewards

Love your city? Giving back, at some point, is part of the grand bargain of citizenship. So many groups in Portland make it rewarding and fun to adopt an urban nook, whether it's a street, natural area, or garden. Or to volunteer for local wildlife: birds, frogs, fish, and amphibians.

Here are the citizen organizations that make the places in this book so enjoyable to explore, along with various ways you can connect with them.

Audubon Society of Portland. If you walk in Portland, you're where the birds are. Volunteer as a Community Science volunteer, monitoring local bird populations, or be a docent in an Audubon sanctuary, or help in the Wildlife Care Center. Or get started turning your yard into a certified Backyard Habitat for wildlife.

Friends of Crystal Springs Rhododendron Garden, along with the Portland chapter of the American Rhododendron Society, maintain the trails, staircases, waterways and plantings in this beautiful place. Work parties are weekly from February through November. Contact csrgvol@gmail.com to volunteer.

SW Trails builds walking routes through Southwest Portland's hills.

Friends of the International Rose Test Garden is a cast of 400 volunteers who prune and dead-head roses, and answer visitors' questions in possibly the most beautiful place in the City. Join their ranks and be part of a Portland icon.

Friends of Lone Fir Cemetery has turned a once neglected city asset into a treasure. Volunteer to educate, maintain, and restore the grounds and monuments. And/or become a member, which includes one free tour a year.

Friends of Marquam Nature Park maintains 200 miles of natural areas and 7 miles of trails, including the Marquam Trail, an early link in the 40-Mile Loop trail system. Ivy removal, an ongoing project, is a satisfying way to volunteer.

Friends of Mt. Tabor Park operates the park's visitor center. Its annual Tar and Trail run raises funds for projects like adding handrails to park staircases. Volunteer to lead tours, like the free tree identification walks. Become a member and support the work.

Friends of Terwilliger maintains areas around historic Terwilliger Parkway. Monthly ivy pulls are an easy way to give back to this iconic linear park.

Human Access Project gets people floating, swimming, and playing in the Willamette River. It also works to build more public access to the river, and holds the annual Big Float and Mayor's Swim. Swim with them, and join the advocacy ranks by becoming a member.

Johnson Creek Watershed Council works to restore the health of this significant urban creek, on its banks and in its floodplain, and in the stream itself. Pull invasives or adopt a street or bioswale for a year, picking up trash, clearing drains, and doing other satisfying work.

Linnton Neighborhood Association/Linnton Frogs. In possibly the city's most unique neighborhood, volunteers beautify this boundary between wilderness and industrial riverbank. And they give an assist to red-legged frogs who endure a Hwy 30 crossing to lay their eggs in the wetlands (and then return to the forest).

Reed Canyon Day happens twice a year, when volunteers from Reed College and anyone who loves the canyon restore and maintain its native vegetation.

SW Trails leads monthly hikes, many of which are on routes, paths, and staircases its volunteers have developed, including the famous 4T Trail. Become a member: for very little money, SW Trails has made a huge difference in enhancing Portland's explorability.

Willamette Riverkeeper advocates for the river that defines Portland.

Be a River Guardian, or a paddle assistant on an educational river tour. Or sign up for regular river cleanups, or represent the river and restoration efforts at local events.

You can also volunteer at events coordinated by the City of Portland. Search for "Stewardship Calendar" at portlandoregon.gov to find upcoming events.

GARDEN STORE

Free Garden Tours
Meet Here
at 1 PM

Tours sponsored by PP&R in conjunction with
the Oregon State University Master Gardeners.

PORTLAND
PARKS & RECREATION
Healthy Parks. Healthy Portland.

Index

About the Author

LAURA O. FOSTER writes about Portland, Oregon and the nearby Columbia River Gorge National Scenic Area. She also writes for Travel Oregon, BikePortland, Friends of the Columbia Gorge, and Portland Parks & Recreation. A former urban-walk guide for the Multnomah Athletic Club, she leads occasional walking tours for nonprofits and local government agencies.

Her explorations of Portland's stairs and hidden paths have been featured on *Oregon Field Guide*, *Oregon Art Beat*, and *AM Northwest*. Her work has been featured on *Portland Monthly*, *Willamette Week*, the *Portland Tribune*, the *Oregonian*, and KBOO's *Between the Covers*. She has been a Portlander since 1989.

Laura blogs about Pacific Northwest places and topics at medium.com/@lauraofoster

SUBSCRIBE TO EVERYTHING WE PUBLISH!

Do you love what Microcosm publishes?

Do you want us to publish more great stuff?

Would you like to receive each new title as it's published?

Subscribe as a BFF to our new titles and we'll mail them all to you as they are released!

$10-30/mo, pay what you can afford. Include your t-shirt size and your birthday for a possible surprise!

microcosmpublishing.com/bff

...AND HELP US GROW YOUR SMALL WORLD!

MORE LOVE FOR PORTLAND:

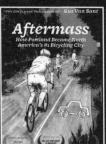